Walk quietly in any direction
and taste the freedom of the mountaineer.
—JOHN MUIR

EVEREST: THE WEST RIDGE

. . . It seemed as though our first view of the Himalaya was to be indefinitely postponed. Again the great cloud screen rose tall above the curve of the world. I was about to turn away disappointedly when a wild thought made me raise my head higher. . . .

They were there. . . .

. . . an arctic continent of the heavens, far above the earth and its girdling clouds: divorced wholly from this planet. The idea of climbing over such distant and delicate tips, the very desire of it, never entered my heart or head. . . .

Had I been born among or in sight of them, I might have been led to worship the infinite beauty they symbolized, but not to set boot on their flanks, or axe on a crest.

—W. H. MURRAY

. . . Everest rises, not so much a peak as a prodigious mountain mass. There is no complication for the eye. The highest of the world's great mountains, it seems, has to make but a single gesture of magnificence to be lord of all, vast in unchallenged and isolated supremacy. To the discerning eye other mountains are visible, giants between twenty-three and twenty-six thousand feet high. Not one of their slenderer heads even reaches their chief's shoulder; beside Everest they escape notice: such is the pre-eminence of the greatest.

—GEORGE LEIGH MALLORY

BARRY BISHOP: Unsoeld and Hornbein approaching the West Ridge
© 1963 National Geographic Society

AL AUTEN: Lingtren

[9

Let others orbit to the inhospitable moon . . .
I shall stay with my gigantic friends
and let them direct my thoughts to eternal truths.
—JOHN MUIR

EVEREST
THE WEST RIDGE

By THOMAS F. HORNBEIN
Photographs from the American Mount Everest Expedition
and by its leader, NORMAN G. DYHRENFURTH
Introduction by WILLIAM E. SIRI

Edited by DAVID BROWER

SIERRA CLUB · SAN FRANCISCO

Acknowledgments

We thank the National Aeronautics and Space Administration for permission to publish L. Gordon Cooper's photograph of the Himalaya and the publishers and copyright holders of the sources listed below for permission to quote excerpts from these sources in this book. We thank the following people for leading us to the quotations we should never have found for ourselves—and the sources of some of which we have not found yet: Genevieve Bancroft, James H. Barbour, Richard J. Berry, Mrs. Nicholas Clinch, Edith A. Coleman, James R. Cox, Dorene Del Fium, May Dornin, Mrs. Herbert Eloesser, Mrs. Richard M. Emerson, Mrs. H. V. Goodell, Everett Austin Goodell, Will Harris, Dr. and Mrs. Hornbein, Leo M. Le Bon, Edwin P. Pister, Margaret K. Seikel, Clarke S. Smith, Jr., Larry Snyder, Wendell H. Stillwell, Ellen M. Sutton, Mrs. Kenneth B. Thompson, Eulalia and Julie Nyce Walker, Eugene H. Walker, Gary Werner.

For assistance on the text itself we are grateful to all the people Dr. Hornbein is grateful to. I owe special appreciation to both Mr. and Mrs. Norman G. Dyhrenfurth for their help in the selection of photographs and to Hugh Barnes and his associates for the special pains they took in translating Kodachrome to lithography. For the final juxtaposition of photographs, text, and excerpts I owe an appreciable debt for invaluable suggestions to my son Kenneth and a great debt to my wife Anne, as well as those who, while I struggled with this book, did without an executive director, father, or husband and carried on anyway.   D.B.

Sources

Buchan, John (Lord Tweedsmuir), *Pilgrim's Way: An Essay in Recollection*, Boston, Houghton Mifflin Company, 1940.

Bishop, Barry C., "How We Climbed Everest," *National Geographic Magazine*, Washington, D.C., October 1963.

Corbet, James Barry, "John Edgar Breitenbach," *The American Alpine Journal*, New York, 1964.

Dittert, René, *Forerunners to Everest*, New York, Harper & Brothers, 1954.

Douglas, William O., *Of Men and Mountains*, New York, Harper & Brothers, 1950.

Emerson, Richard M., "Masherbrum 1960," *Sierra Club Bulletin*, San Francisco, December 1960.

Gesner, Conrad, *On the Admiration of Mountains*, San Francisco, The Grabhorn Press, 1937.

Green, Vivian, *The Swiss Alps*, London, B. T. Batsford, Ltd., 1961.

Hagen, Toni, Günter-Oskar Dyhrenfurth, Christoph Von Fürer-Haimendorf, and Erwin Schneider, *Mount Everest*, London, Oxford University Press, 1963.

Hammarskjöld, Dag, *Markings*, New York, Alfred A. Knopf, 1964.

Ortega y Gasset, José, *The Dehumanization of Art and Notes on the Novel*, Princeton, Princeton University Press, 1948.

———, *Man and People*, New York, W. W. Norton & Company, Inc., 1957.

Pope Pius XI in Captain John Noel's *The Story of Everest*, Boston, Little, Brown and Company, 1927.

Rébuffat, Gaston, *Mont Blanc to Everest*, London, Thames and Hudson, 1956.

Rey, Guido, *Peaks and Precipices*, New York, Dodd, Mead and Company, 1914.

Stephen, Leslie, *The Playground of Europe*, London, Longmans, Green, and Co., 1871.

Stuck, Hudson, *The Ascent of Denali (Mount McKinley)*, New York, Charles Scribner's Sons, 1914, as quoted by Rébuffat in *Mont Blanc to Everest*, which see.

Thoreau, Henry David, *The Maine Woods*, New York, Thomas Y. Crowell & Co., 1906.

Harrer, Heinrich, *The White Spider*, New York, E. P. Dutton, 1960.

Heller, Erich, *The Disinherited Mind*, Cambridge, Eng., Bowes & Bowes, 1952.

Herron, Rand, in Elizabeth Knowlton's, *The Naked Mountain*, which see.

Kipling, Rudyard, from "The Explorer."

Knowlton, Elizabeth, *The Naked Mountain*, New York, G. P. Putnam's Sons, 1933.

Lunn, Sir Arnold Henry Moore, *Mountains of Memory*, Longon, Hollis and Carter, 1938.

Mallory, George Leigh, in Lieut.-Col. C. K. Howard-Bury's *Mount Everest, The Reconnaissance, 1921*, New York, Longmans, Green and Co., 1922.

Mummery, Albert Frederick, *My Climbs in the Alps and Caucasus*, London, T. Fisher Unwin, 1895.

Murray, W. H., *The Scottish Himalayan Expedition*, London, J. M. Dent & Sons Ltd., 1951.

Noyce, Wilfrid, "Why Men Seek Adventure," *Horizon*, September 1958.

Tietjens, Eunice, "The Most Sacred Mountain," 1917, quoted from *Anthology of Magazine Verse*, New York, Braithewaite and Carpenter, 1958.

Tolkien, J. R. R., *The Fellowship of the Ring* (vol. 1 of *The Lord of the Rings*), Boston, Houghton Mifflin Company, 1954.

———, *The Two Towers* (vol II of *The Lord of the Rings*), Boston, Houghton Mifflin Company, 1954.

Ullman, James Ramsey, *High Conquest*, New York, J. B. Lippincott Company, New York, 1941.

Whitman, Walt, from "Song of the Open Road."

Young, Geoffrey Winthrop, *High Hills*, London, Methuen and Co., Ltd., 1927.

———, *Mountains with a Difference*, London, Eyre & Spottiswoode Ltd., 1951.

Younghusband, Sir Francis, in Lieut.-Col. C. K. Howard-Bury's *Mount Everest, The Reconnaissance, 1921*, New York, Longmans, Green and Co., 1922.

Publisher's Note: The book is set in Centaur and Arrighi by Mackenzie & Harris, Inc., San Francisco. It was printed on Champion Kromekote by Barnes Press, Inc., New York City. It is single sheet collated and is bound in Columbia Mills' Sampson linen by Sendor Bindery, New York City. The design is by David Brower.

PUBLICATIONS COMMITTEE, 1964–1965

AUGUST FRUGÉ, *Chairman*, GEORGE MARSHALL, *Vice Chairman*
MARTIN LITTON, WILLIAM E. SIRI (*ex officio, President of the club*)
CHARLES B. HUESTIS, CLIFFORD J. RUDDEN, *Controller*
DAVID BROWER, *Executive Director*, HUGH NASH, *Secretary*

The Sierra Club, founded in 1892 by John Muir, has devoted itself to the study and protection of national scenic resources, particularly those of mountain regions. All Sierra Club publications are part of the nonprofit effort the club carries on as a public trust. The club is affiliated with the International Union for Conservation, the Natural Resources Council of America, and the Federation of Western Outdoor Clubs. There are chapters in California, the Pacific Northwest, the Great Basin, the Southwest, the Great Lakes region, and on the Atlantic seaboard. Participation is invited in the program to enjoy and preserve wilderness, wildlife, forests, and streams. *Address: Mills Tower, San Francisco; 25 West 45th Street, New York; 710 Dupont Circle Building, Washington, D.C.*

L. GORDON COOPER: Himalayas in the India-Nepal-Tibet border area
(From the Faith 7 spacecraft, orbit 9, 30N, 79E, altitude 100 miles)

Photographs

Contents

A NOTE ON THE MAKE-UP OF THE BOOK
There are many important advantages in lithographing color photographs on the highly calendared side of a sheet and single-sheet collation of the book; but there is at least one disadvantage—the requirement that there be no less than one page of text for each page of illustration. Kromekote was accordingly a difficult taskmaster at times. The marriage between Tom Hornbein's West Side Story and a representative selection of photographs from the Expedition (and by Norman Dyhrenfurth from other expeditions of his) does not always run an obvious course. Dr. Hornbein was primarily concerned about how the West Ridge was won; we were concerned also with the lower terrain and man's achievements there. Accordingly, there are occasional editorial interludes, duly flagged, especially at the beginning. We hope they will be pleasant interludes and are grateful for the writings we borrowed to try to make them so.

Chronology

1963

February 3: Bulk of Expedition departs San Francisco by air.

February 13: Arrive Kathmandu, Nepal.

February 20: Depart Kathmandu, begin march from Banepa to Panchkal on first day.

February 21: Panchkal to Dolalghat. Jim Ullman returns to Kathmandu.

March 5: Puijan.

March 9-14: Thangboche, 13,000 feet, for acclimatization.

March 16-19: Lobuje, 16,000 feet, for more acclimatization.

March 21: Base Camp established at head of Khumbu Glacier, 17,800 feet.

March 22: First probe into Icefall by Nawang Gombu, Lute Jerstad, Willi Unsoeld, and Jim Whittaker.

March 23: Jake Breitenbach killed.

April 2: Advance Base established in Western Cwm at 21,350 feet.

April 7-13: Reconnaissance of West Ridge to 25,100 feet by Barry Bishop, Dave Dingman, Tom Hornbein, Willi Unsoeld.

April 16: South Col, 26,200 feet, reached by Lute Jerstad, Dick Pownall, Chotari, and Nima Tenzing; one month earlier than past expeditions.

April 16-May 13: Winch operations on West Shoulder by Al Auten, Barry Corbet, Dick Emerson, Willi Unsoeld, Tashi, and Nima Tenzing.

April 27: First South Col team of Ang Dawa, Norman Dyhrenfurth, Nawang Gombu, and Jim Whittaker depart Advance Base for the summit.

April 28: Second South Col team of Barry Bishop, Girmi Dorje, Lute Jerstad, and Dick Pownall starts up.

April 29: Final support and Lhotse team of Dave Dingman and Barry Prather leave Advance Base.

May 1: Nawang Gombu and Jim Whittaker reach the summit of Everest at 1 P.M. by way of the South Col route. Very high winds. Norman Dyhrenfurth and Ang Dawa in photographic support reach 28,000 feet before returning to Camp VI. All four spend a second night in high camp before going down.

May 2: All parties descend, second summit team helping the first team down from the South Col.

May 15: Camp 4W established, 25,100 feet, at base of West Ridge.

May 16-17, night of: Windstorm flattens Camp 4W. Al Auten, Barry Corbet, Tom Hornbein, and Willi Unsoeld retire to 3W to find Dick Emerson who has spent the night bivouacking in a crevasse on way up to 3W.

May 18-19: West Ridgers recuperate at 3W while Barry Bishop and Lute Jerstad, then Dave Dingman and Girmi Dorje depart Advance Base for South Col.

May 20: West Ridgers reoccupy Camp 4W.

May 21: Barry Bishop and Lute Jerstad to Camp VI, 27,450 feet, above South Col. Long carry from Camp 4W to establish 5W at 25,250 feet. Route pioneered by Barry Corbet and Al Auten. Carry by Ang Dorje, Ila Tsering, Passang Tendi, Tenzing Nindra, and Tenzing Gyalsto. Dick Emerson, Tom Hornbein, and Willi Unsoeld come last.

May 22: Barry Bishop and Lute Jerstad reach summit of Everest via South Col route at 3:30 P.M. Willi Unsoeld and Tom Hornbein arrive three hours later up West Ridge, then descend toward South Col. The two parties unite after dark and spend night out at 28,000 feet.

May 23: The four descending are met by Dave Dingman and Girmi Dorje above Camp VI, then led by Dave Dingman down to Advance Base, arriving at 10:30 P.M.

May 24: Last of Expedition descends to Base Camp.

May 26: Barry Bishop and Willi Unsoeld transported from Namche Bazar to Shanta Bhavan hospital in Kathmandu by helicopter.

June 9: Rest of Expedition reaches Kathmandu.

Members, American Mount Everest Expedition

Allen (Al) C. Auten: 36, Denver, Colorado; Assistant Editor of *Design News*; Responsible for Expedition radio communications.

Barry (Barrel) C. Bishop: 31, Washington, D.C.; Photographer, National Geographic Society; Expedition still photographer.

John (Jake) E. Breitenbach: 27, Jackson, Wyoming; Mountain guide and part owner of mountaineering and ski equipment store, Grand Tetons.

James Barry Corbet: 26, Jackson, Wyoming; Mountain guide, ski instructor, and part owner of mountaineering and ski equipment store, Grand Tetons.

David (Dave) L. Dingman, M.D.: 26, Baltimore, Maryland; Resident in surgery; Second medical officer of Expedition.

Daniel (Dan) E. Doody: 29, North Granford, Connecticut; Photographer by profession and for Expedition.

Norman G. Dyhrenfurth: 44, Santa Monica, California; Motion picture photographer and director; Expedition organizer, leader, and film producer.

Richard (Dick) M. Emerson, Ph.D.: 38, Cincinnati, Ohio; Assistant Professor of Sociology, University of Cincinnati; Expedition logistical planner, and head of sociological study on motivation.

Thomas (Tom) F. Hornbein, M.D.: 32, San Diego, California; Physician; Responsible for Expedition oxygen equipment and planning.

Luther (Lute) G. Jerstad: 26, Eugene, Oregon; Speech instructor, University of Oregon, and mountain guide, Mount Rainier.

James (Jim) Lester, Ph.D.: 35, Berkeley, California; Clinical psychologist; Studied psychological aspects of stress during Expedition.

Maynard M. Miller, Ph.D.: 41, East Lansing, Michigan; Associate Professor of geology (glaciology, etc.), Michigan State University; Research in glaciology and geomorphology of the Everest region.

Richard (Dick) Pownall: 35, Denver, Colorado; High school physical education instructor and ski instructor; Expedition food planner.

Barry (Bear, Balu) W. Prather: 23, Ellensburg, Washington; Aeronautics engineer; Assistant to Maynard Miller in geological research.

Gilbert (Gil) Roberts, M.D.: 28, Berkeley, California; Physician; Responsible for medical planning and problems of Expedition.

James (Jimmy) Owen M. Roberts: 45, Kathmandu, Nepal; Lt. Colonel (retired), British Army; Responsible for Expedition transport and porter and Sherpa planning.

William (Will) E. Siri: 44, Richmond, California; Medical physicist; Deputy leader of Expedition in charge of scientific program and conduction of physiological research on altitude acclimatization.

James (Jim) Ramsey Ullman: 55, Boston, Massachusetts; Writer; Official chronicler of Expedition as author of *Americans on Everest*.

William (Willi) F. Unsoeld, Ph.D.: 36, Corvallis, Oregon; Assistant Professor, Department of Philosophy and Religion, Oregon State University, on leave as deputy Peace Corps representative in Nepal; Expedition planner and leader.

James (Jim) W. Whittaker: 34, Redmond, Washington; Manager of mountaineering equipment store, Seattle, Washington; Responsible for Expedition equipment planning.

JAMES LESTER: Girl in doorway, Kathmandu

For Gene
who was willing to give so much

Preface

Climbing Everest is one thing, writing about it quite another. Still the reasons for writing seemed compelling enough to overcome doubts of my ability and a yearning for the privacy a mountaineer tends to prize so highly. Besides which, as I soon learned, Everest was not a private affair. It belonged to many men.

And so therefore did our story. Realizing this, I found myself challenged to convey something of the less dramatic but more deeply meaningful reality of an expedition, using the climb not as an end in itself but as a stage on which men could act, and interact.

This is the West Ridge story. It is only a small part of what was accomplished by the American Mount Everest Expedition, but the rest—the two ascents by way of the South Col route, the scientific endeavours—has been told elsewhere, most powerfully by James Ramsey Ullman in *Americans on Everest*. Hopefully his account will justify my gross omissions. To narrow scope even further, this is a personal account, seen through the eyes, and the bias, of one of a team of twenty. Obviously much more could be said, but the West Ridge is all that I personally experienced; it is all that I am qualified to write about.

My goal is to place the drama, the hardship, the toiling up windswept heights into a setting of day-to-day reality, a setting of grubby unbathed living, of hours of sweaty boredom and moments of fun or aloneness for introspection, a setting where men are human beings, nothing more . . . and nothing less.

In this sense a mountaineering expedition is like a marriage. Close living for many weeks rubs away the veneer. A man may appear before his companions burdened by an excess of faults and annoying habits that challenge the joy of daily living. Weaknesses show, but also strengths; personal ambitions, but also the ability to compromise. The result, to my taste, is always for the better, and when the team is right (here the skill came in Norman's choosing) the experience becomes more meaningful day by day.

Stress is inevitable in such a situation, particularly when goals diverge. To ignore disagreement and the ability of individuals to forge from compromise that which was accomplished is to ignore much of the accomplishment. This is what I have attempted to portray.

The story is written as I experienced it at the time, not as I feel looking back upon it now. In recapturing feelings and reconstructing events, in separating fact from bias, I have been helped immensely by my diary and letters home and by tape recordings of radio conversations and group discussions made during the expedition. Most of the dialogue of group discussions and all the radio conversations on the mountain are taken directly from these tapes with editing only where necessary for clarity and pace.

In many ways the writing of this book resembles the climbing of the mountain it is about. It was as difficult, and, like Everest, it remained so to the last. It evoked the same pleasurable feelings of finality as the end came near. And, like the climbing of Everest, this account results from the work and caring of many besides myself.

Norman Dyhrenfurth started it by conceiving the expedition. His dream brought reality to the dreams of those who joined him. He will have to sense my gratitude for the opportunity, for words cannot do it justice.

In the writing Dick Emerson has provided a constant and solid belay. He shared generously of his own ideas and carried my thoughts to depths that would otherwise have remained unplumbed. His wife, Pat, typed and edited incisively. She and Twink Stern tried to keep my writing honest with my philosophies, as best they could understand either. Joan Green typed early in the game when the idea was still a fear, and Chuck Huestis helped to tie loose ends as the effort neared completion. Dave Brower's confidence when there was little cause for confidence and his skill in polishing what finally came were still less than his contribution of his son, Ken, who helped put chaos in order when time grew short. To all these people I owe far more than thanks.

And to the team, about whom this story is written. Though some are here more than others, in the event of which this is just a small part such distinctions did not exist.

The one that thanks miss entirely is my wife, Gene. The hours of writing taken from her are unrecoverable, particularly when added to the five months of complete separation from her and our children, a time when for her the challenge of survival must have been a chore.

T. H.

Seattle
September 17, 1965

Foreword

"If we can pull it off," Norman Dyhrenfurth said of the West Ridge, "it would be the biggest possible thing still to be accomplished in Himalayan mountaineering." This judgment came from the man best qualified to make it. He was leading the American Mount Everest Expedition when he said it; he had already climbed in many lands, had been on four previous Himalayan expeditions including the Swiss expedition to Everest, and he had been dreaming of the West Ridge for years. Genetics had a role as well; his father had organized and led international Himalayan expeditions and his mother had participated too.

The importance of the West Ridge was clear to Tom Hornbein and Willi Unsoeld; they knew that there should be a book about it soon after they completed their unique traverse of the top of the world. We knew, at the annual banquet of the American Alpine Club in Philadelphia in December 1963, that there should be a Sierra Club Exhibit Format book on the American Everest Expedition before Norman Dyhrenfurth's illustrated lecture about it ended. We did not know, however, how good a marriage the two projects would make.

We talked about a book in three parts: About the approach, the people and the environment the Expedition met as it started out. About the contest, man versus rock and ice and versus his own weaknesses, shored up with his own inner strength—not the nuts-and-bolts story of the climb but something reaching deeper. About the prospect of man and mountains in general, one that would review the relationship from the time man learned to accept the mountains' challenge as a game. The finest Himalayan photographs we could find would be paired with the most moving excerpts of text others could find. Perhaps such a book would reveal the survival value to man of the force within him that sends him off to summits.

Long talks with Dick Emerson, whom I had known since Mountain Troop days, with Will Siri, Sierra Club president, and with Norman Dyhrenfurth all pointed to Tom Hornbein as author. He agreed to try, while protesting "But they don't know what I'm going to say." It worked out.

The American Mount Everest Expedition Board of Directors lent a shoulder—Norman's—to the Battle of the Book, which is quite a story in itself. We won't go into it except to give credit to the flexibility of men—the kind that gets them to physical summits—that let the book become a book.

It wouldn't have happened if Norman Dyhrenfurth hadn't wanted it to. A professional photographer himself, in addition to being a mountaineer extraordinary and leader of the Expedition, he could advise best on illustrations. He wanted us to

do a book because we had been braver with illustrations than commercial publishers can dare to be and we had got away with it, nonprofit but still solvent. He sent out the call to the Expedition members and the Kodachromes came in—some ten thousand of them. Norman went through them all, and his and my initial scrutiny narrowed the selection to five hundred, only one out of five of which we could afford to use. I looked, stared, and gazed and the number wouldn't reduce. There would have to be two or three volumes, not one. There still could be.

For this volume, we tried not to use so many photographs that they would begin to cancel each other out or make the book too expensive. As a rule, if a photograph wasn't worth a full page, we left it out. We wanted the photographs to be strong, to say something, and to have room to say it in.

We are pleased, of course, when American mountaineers do well; but we are also pleased when any mountaineers do well in what is still mankind's frontier, even as space is. That a given flag should wave long from the high point on the border between Nepal and Tibet isn't too important. Certainly not to this book. There has been much detailed talk about men and mountains in this decade; there needs also to be a suggestion of what mountains have meant to universal man over a long span of time. A great deal has been written in the past two centuries, and a little was recorded before that. Some of the writing has been exceptionally good. In my own reading through the years, a paragraph, or a line, has picked me up and transported me now and then. Others looking at the literature subjectively must likewise have been picked up and sent somewhere by words about mountains. We asked in the June *Sierra Club Bulletin* if people would care to submit "paragraphs to be turned on by" from their own experience to be used in the Everest book. No request in the *SCB* ever brought more response. The Sierra Club was still the alpine club John Muir was asked to help organize. As with the color photographs, we found ourselves with enough quotations for two volumes or three. How to appose paragraphs with photographs, as words to music, may be an exact craft; if so we haven't learned it but we keep trying different ways, mindful always that one man's counterpoint may be another's dissonance. If the apposition works, the whole is greater than the sum.

It is appropriate, I think, that this book should appear when the present president of the Sierra Club is, like the first president, a mountaineer. John Muir, having walked a thousand miles to the Gulf, also explored Alaska and climbed peaks in the Sierra Nevada. Will Siri, with five expeditions behind him, four of which he led, was deputy leader in charge of research for the American Mount Everest Expedition and is the logical man to introduce this book. Many of his contributions to the Sierra Club aren't readily apparent, among them what he has done to keep the club's directors optimistic enough about club books and the club's executive director free enough of other duties to put this one together. No one who has not been a president of the Sierra Club is likely to know how much more difficult it is than Everest. There are a dozen frays to be joined at any given moment as man's overenthusiastic technology tends to destroy too much of the environment that the community of life—including man's—depends upon for survival.

The transcending conservation battles being waged as this book took shape were to save Grand Canyon from being dammed by the Bureau of Reclamation, the last redwoods of national park potential from being logged by private industry, and the Northern Cascades of Washington from the same fate at Forest Service hands. Meanwhile San Francisco Bay was being filled too much, reactors, power lines, and freeways were being pressed upon coastal sections in California that shouldn't have them, a principal wildlife-producing area in Alaska was being threatened by the Corps of Engineers, Storm King Mountain by Consolidated Edison, Central Park by an unnecessary bar and restaurant, and so on and on in the malignant growth of blind progress. Exactly what, people asked when they saw this book begin, was the Sierra Club expecting to save in the Everest region? Wild habitat for the Abominable Snowman, I would answer—then remind them that we are still a mountaineering organization, even as we were when we started, and it is all right to enjoy mountains from time to time as well as to worry about what is happening to them. We would help them enjoy Everest so long as they would share the worrying in their odd moments. That is part of the price of this book—and the only reason a volunteer, unpaid president's time could be spared from his conservation obligations in order to put the book in context.

Unlike any other Sierra Club book, this one has depended largely upon 35 mm color transparencies for illustration. Others in the Exhibit Format Series have rarely drawn upon anything smaller than 2¼ x 2¼, have relied chiefly upon 4 x 5's, and have luxuriated occasionally in 5 x 7's and 8 x 10's. Some detail must necessarily be lost in 35 mm, particularly if the camera is hand-held. Heavy tripods and cameras are not popular on Everest with amateurs or anyone else; 35 mm, for all the drawbacks, is a boon. It can be shot quickly when it must be, or with great precision and extraordinary care about composition when there is time. We use both kinds of photographs. Gordon Cooper's Faith 7 transparency was 2¼ x 2¼; all others are 35 mm, and

we are grateful for the extraordinary interpretation of Everest country and people they have made possible.

Dr. Hornbein, we learned, is an anesthesiologist who doesn't like or want to write but who did want to tell about the climb. On the post-Expedition lecture circuit he had called it "West Side Story." That might be the subtitle of the book, he thought for a while. He also suggested "How the West Was Won" and "The One Less Traveled by," but conservatism won out, and for the most exciting story an Exhibit Format book will ever tell we chose the most austere title.

His diary, his letters to his wife, tapes of expedition discussions and radio conversations—these were his raw materials. More important, he was there and his own personal built-in perceiving apparatus was highly sensitive. Most important, he is honest; he likes spades to be called spades no matter who is doing the calling. I think he wanted a do-it-yourself mountaineering book, one in which he would give the facts as directly as he could, but not too explicitly. He would let you figure out who was right and wrong then and now, but no recriminations please, because this is the way it was and you could have been right or wrong too, and you don't have to be right. It goes without saying Tom Hornbein is a superb climber—and it would have to go without saying if I were to give him a chance to edit this line. Combine his attributes and you have a story that you never quite heard before about mountains. You are reminded that each man in unique. We are compounded of dust and the light of a star, Loren Eiseley says; and if you look hard at the frontispiece, Barry Bishop's photograph of Tom Hornbein and Willi Unsoeld approaching the West Ridge—if you keep looking at it as I have in the course of putting the book together, you will be able to see something phenomenal. They have climbed off the foreground snow by now, so you must look high, on the rock just below the summit. It isn't too hard for an imaginative person to see there a momentary pulsing of a pinpoint of light.

The light of a star. What is it that enabled dust to carry it there? How could an impossibly complicated array of cells ever organize at all, much less seek out such a place to go? This inclination to inquire, this drive to go higher than need be, this innate ability to carry it off, this radiance in the heart when it happens, however brief in the infinite eternity, whether you do it or I, or Tom and Willi, makes us grateful for the genius that man has and for the beautiful planet he has to live on.

DAVID BROWER

Berkeley, California
September 9, 1965

We do not feel proud enough of being alive.

—GOEFFREY WINTHROP YOUNG

Introduction

OTHER MOUNTAINS share with Everest a history of adventure, glory, and tragedy, but only Everest is the highest place on earth. More than two-thirds of the earth's atmosphere lies below its summit, and for an unacclimatized man without oxygen, the top of the mountain is more endurable than outer space by only two or three minutes. The primitive, often brutal struggle to reach its top is an irresistible challenge to our built-in need for adventure. But more than this, Everest became, with the first attempt to scale its ridges, a universal symbol of human courage and endurance; an ultimate test of man's body and spirit.

The discovery in 1852 that Peak XV was the highest mountain in the world emerged from a page of routine survey calculations. When a clerk in the Trigonometric Survey of India offices excitedly informed his superior of his discovery, a careful check of his calculations, which were based on observations made three years earlier, confirmed his claim and the summit was set at 29,002 feet. (Careful modern observations have settled on an elevation of 29,028 feet, the value now generally accepted.) Peak XV now rated more distinction than a file number and was given the name Mount Everest after the first surveyor general of India, Sir George Everest. There was no way then of knowing that the Tibetans long ago recognized it as the greatest of mountains and called it Chomo-longma, Goddess Mother of the World.

For sixty-nine years following the clerk's exciting discovery little more could be learned about Mount Everest. It stood astride the Nepalese-Tibetan border, remote and inaccessible. Nepal and Tibet were tightly sealed against foreigners and hostile to intruders. From India, Mount Everest was all but hidden from view by lesser but nearer peaks.

Not until 1921, after years of negotiation, was permission coaxed from the Tibetan government and a reconnaissance expedition launched from Darjeeling. The route circled 400 miles over the high, windy Tibetan plateau to reach the north side of Mount Everest at the head of the Rongbuk Glacier. In the course of this first reconnaissance the most famous of early Everest climbers, George Leigh Mallory found the key to the route on Everest by his discovery of the East Rongbuk Glacier, from which the North Col (23,000 feet) could be climbed. All succeeding British expeditions before World War II were compelled to make the long, exhausting trek across the Tibetan plateau to the north side of Everest. The first full-scale attempt on Everest was launched by the British the following year. For this early period of high-altitude climbing Geoffrey Bruce and George Finch performed an incredible feat in climbing to more than 27,000 feet before they were turned back by wind and exhaustion. The 1922 expedition ended in failure and tragedy, but the route to the summit of Everest was now clear. Spring of 1924 saw another strong British climbing party struggle to the North Col and force its way up the Northeast ridge of Everest. For the third time Mallory, whose name was to become almost synonymous with that of the mountain that obsessed him, returned to Everest determined that nothing could turn him back. E. F. Norton and T. H. Somervell, however, were to make the first summit attempt and in doing so reached a new record height of more than 28,000 feet, which placed them at the Great Couloir directly below the summit.

Mallory and his young companion, Andrew Irvine, now made their bid for the summit, with N. E. Odell climbing one day behind them in support. From the highest camp at more than 27,000 feet, Odell saw Mallory and Irvine briefly as they ascended a prominent step high on the main East Ridge before the scene was obscured by clouds. At that point they were unaccountably four or five hours behind schedule. The winds that took over Everest that afternoon continued without letup for days. In a remarkable tour de force, Odell searched the whole route from the North Col to more than 27,000 feet for signs of the missing climbers before he was driven back by the storm.

Speculation on the fate of Mallory and Irvine continues to this day. Did they fall and now lie entombed in the Rongbuk Glacier? Did they perish from cold and exhaustion high on the East Ridge? Or did they reach the summit? It is tempting to think they did and that they still lie frozen in bivouac where they were overtaken by darkness and storm on the descent. It is possible they made the same decision as that made later by Hornbein and Unsoeld to push on to the summit despite the late hour and difficulties. If they did, they were less lucky than the Americans. Perhaps on 49 nights out of 50 the cold winds raging over Everest make such a decision fatal.

A lapse of nine years brought a new generation of British climbers to Everest. Two successive summit teams in 1933 were turned back, like their predecessors, just beyond 28,000 feet. Only a reconnaissance was possible in 1935 because of frustrating delays in securing permission from Tibet. In 1936 a powerful expedition was defeated by storms and avalanches before it ever set foot on the mountain. Two years later, two summit attempts by the 1938 British expedition were again frustrated by the seemingly impenetrable barrier at 28,000 feet. The first chapter of the struggle for Everest's summit was brought to a close by the outbreak of World War II.

After centuries of isolation, Nepal in 1949 opened its border to foreign visitors. Everest was now accessible by a direct, low-level route from India, and the scene of activity shifted to Everest's south side. Light reconnaissance parties pioneered the new trail to Everest in 1950 and 1951. They also saw that the only possible route onto the mountain was a narrow, hazardous icefall rising from the Khumbu Glacier to the high valley of ice, the Western Cwm, between Everest and the Lhotse-Nuptse Ridge. Permission for Everest was now on a first-come-first-served basis and the Swiss were ready first. On their first try in the spring of 1952 the Swiss pioneered the whole route via the South Col and they nearly reached the summit. Raymond Lambert and Tenzing Norgay ascended the Southeast Ridge within 800 feet. In the fall they returned for another attempt but were forced by intense cold, high winds, and short days to retreat before reaching the former high point. It was as a member of this Expedition that Norman Dyhrenfurth became hopelessly addicted to Everest. Eleven years later he would organize and lead the American expedition. The following spring, 1953, the British were ready. R. C. Evans and T. D. Bourdillon made the first attempt, and might have succeeded but for the failure of their intricate, closed-circuit oxygen apparatus. They reached the South Summit, only 300 feet below the main summit, and no great climbing difficulties lay ahead. Using the more reliable though less efficient open-circuit apparatus, the next team set out from the South Col. On May 29, 1953, Edmund Hillary and Tenzing Norgay reached the summit. Everest had at last been climbed.

If it lost any of the luster it had as an unclimbed peak, Everest still remained the most alluring of goals for climbers. It was, after all, still the highest mountain in the world. Dyhrenfurth returned to the mountain in the fall of 1955 with a strong but small team, too small in resources to tackle Everest; so they turned their attention to Lhotse. Once again, as in the fall of 1952, the merciless autumn winds and cold made high altitudes untenable. When the Swiss returned in 1956, it was to make a clean sweep of Everest. In near perfect weather four men reached the summit: Ernest Schmeid and Jurg Marmet on one day; Hans-Rudolf von Gunten and Adolf Reist the next. As if Everest were not enough, two members of the expedition also made the first ascent of Lhotse (27,890 feet).

Two large, well-equipped Indian expeditions were to challenge Everest before the Americans arrived on the scene. Both expeditions were brutally mauled by almost continuous storms and high-velocity winds. Despite this, the first Indian expedition in 1960, with Nawang Gombu leading the summit team, forced its way to 28,300 feet. The second expedition in 1962 pushed on to 28,600 feet before it too was blown from the mountain. There was activity on the north side of Everest as well. The Chinese in 1960 launched a full-scale assault from the Rongbuk Glacier via the North Col route of the early British expeditions. The claim that two Chinese climbers, Wang Fu Chou and Chu Yin Hua, together with Kobu, a Tibetan, reached the summit has been questioned. The climbers said they arrived at the summit at 1:50 in the morning of May 25, 1960, the same day the Indian summit team on the south side was turned back by fierce winds. Other attempts of sorts have been made on the north side. Maurice Wilson, an Englishman driven by fanatical faith in a divine vision, tried it alone in 1934 and died at the foot of the ice cliffs of the North Col. An American, Woodrow Wilson Sayre, and three companions, none of whom were experienced climbers, crossed secretly into Tibet from Nepal in 1962 to make an unauthorized attempt on Everest from the north. An intense personal drive combined with a sequence of incredibly lucky circumstances that all but surpasses belief permitted Sayre to reach 25,000 feet and live to tell about it. Everest is sometimes merciful as well as cruel.

By the time the Americans arrived, Everest had been climbed by six men, possibly nine, conceivably eleven. The routes on two of its three ridges were well established. The third, the West Ridge, had been given only passing notice by earlier expeditions and dismissed as hopeless. No one knew if Americans were yet ready to climb Everest by any route but we were determined that they would not fail, as we had on Makalu, for want of equipment, funds, and even food. The Expedition consequently was large by American mountaineering standards, but so were its aims. The addition of Lhotse and Nuptse to the original list of goals meant a large climbing team. Moreover, the Expedition was conceived and organized from the outset as a joint mountaineering-scientific venture and this added still more to the manpower, impedimenta, and cost. The aims were also made more difficult, if not expanded, by the abandonment of Lhotse and Nuptse for the unexplored West Ridge of Everest. During three hectic years of preparation, the expedition grew constantly in size and ambitions. By the time Dyhrenfurth brought his creation to the foot of Everest, there were nineteen American members, a British transport officer, a Nepalese liaison officer, some 47 Sherpas, more than nine hundred porters bearing twenty-seven tons of material, and six separate scientific programs.

American expeditions had been shoestring affairs in the past and doubtless will continue to be so in the future. The Everest Expedition was different for no other reason than the determination and genius of Norman Dyhrenfurth. He brought his dream of a powerful, well-equipped American expedition to reality. During the three-year struggle, I often marveled at his total dedication to the task, and even more at his eloquent persuasiveness—and astonishing success—in seeking support for the venture. Supporting his natural talent for planning and organizing the expedition was an intimate knowledge of the Himalaya possessed by few men and no other American. In the end, the expedition's achievements matched its ambitions. James Whittaker and Nawang Gombu, and later Luther Jerstad and Barry Bishop, reached the summit by the South Col route; Tom Hornbein and Willi Unsoeld successfully pioneered a new and difficult route on the West Ridge; and the scientific programs brought back new insight into the nature of high-altitude glaciers and a wealth of information on man's physiological machinery, his mental processes, and group behavior.

The seed of the idea of challenging Everest by way of the West Ridge was planted by Dyhrenfurth early in the Expedition's formative stage. It lay dormant until we were well on the road to the mountain, marching over the foothills of the Himalaya, before it grew into an unwavering dedication in the minds of Tom Hornbein, Willi Unsoeld, and their old climbing companions, Corbet, Emerson, and Breitenbach. Pioneering a new route on Everest excited everyone's imagination, for a high reconnaissance of the Ridge would be a gratifying mountaineering achievement even though it fell short of the summit. But there is a vast gulf between success and the best of tries short of it. The Expedition would be a failure in nearly every sense if the whole of its effort had been expended in a courageous but unsuccessful attempt via the Ridge. The moral and contractual commitments we had accepted to make the Expedition possible made the decision clear. Until the summit was reached by the South Col—the surer way—no large-scale diversions, however attractive, should jeopardize this effort. The larger part of the team was no less dedicated to climbing Everest by the South Col than were others to exploring the West Ridge.

There was no doubt in our minds that following the ascent of Everest, the resources of the Expedition would be diverted to the West Ridge. The opportunity could not be passed over, for the Expedition possessed a rare asset: strong, skillful climbers who were totally dedicated to the task. Nevertheless, the patience of the West Ridgers would be tried in the weeks before May 1, when Whittaker and Gombu hoisted themselves and their flagpole onto the summit of Everest.

Inevitably the Expedition's large size evoked the ancient but still favorite subject for debate among mountaineers: the merits of small versus large expeditions. The subject is heavily crusted with subjective values and consequently conducive to strong convictions, vigorous debate, and, of course, is impossible to spoil with definitive conclusions. Climbers tend to be rugged individualists. To them climbing is not a sport in the true sense, least of all an organized sport. Rather, it is a deep personal experience enjoyed in its fullest only when shared with a few close companions. Large expeditions bring with them some of the trappings and restraints of organized society that the climber would just as soon leave behind.

Nevertheless, the large expeditions have, for the most part, offered the only opportunity to challenge the greatest Himalayan peaks with any reasonable expectation of success. No serious climber could resist the call to join such an expedition no matter how strong his feelings about its size and multiplicity of nonmountaineering commitments. If his convictions are strong, he cannot help feeling at times a conflict between his obligations to the leader and the highly personal satisfactions and freedoms he seeks in mountaineering.

The ascent of the West Ridge and with it the traverse of Everest constitute one of the most astonishing feats in Himalayan mountaineering history. The meeting near the summit of two successful teams from opposite sides of the mountain, and their survival of a bivouac at 28,000 feet without oxygen, shelter, or food, added both intentional and unintentional embellishments to an already unique feat. Tom Hornbein has given us a stirring account of this great episode in Himalayan climbing. Everest can be an overwhelming experience that is more complex and deeply felt than simply the exposure for several months to discomfort, exhausting effort, uncertainty, and awesome scenery. The ascent of the West Ridge as seen through the eyes and mind of Hornbein brings clearly into focus the human as well as the physical struggle that is a part of climbing a great peak. In his intensely personal story, Hornbein shows a subtle insight into the feelings and impressions, the hopes and frustrations of those who would climb Everest. Each responds differently to the experience; but the country, the mountain, and the intense struggle leave deep, lasting marks—some that are scars hard to live with, and some that a man would never wish to lose.

—WILLIAM E. SIRI

It was vast, Titanic, and such as man never inhabits. Some part of the beholder, even some vital part, seems to escape through the loose grating of his ribs as he ascends. He is more lone than you can imagine. There is less of substantial thought and fair understanding in him than in the plains where men inhabit. His reason is dispersed and shadowy, more thin and subtle, like the air. Vast, Titanic, inhuman Nature has got him at disadvantage, caught him alone, and pilfers him of some of his divine faculty. She does not smile on him as in the plains. She seems to say sternly, Why came ye here before your time. This ground is not prepared for you. Is it not enough that I smile in the valleys? I have never made this soil for thy feet, this air for thy breathing, these rocks for thy neighbors. I cannot pity nor fondle thee here, but forever relentlessly drive thee hence to where I *am* kind. Why seek me where I have not called thee, and then complain because you find me but a stepmother? Shouldst thou freeze or starve, or shudder thy life away, here is no shrine, nor altar, nor access to my ear.

—HENRY DAVID THOREAU

Mallory and a Perspective

T. H. Somervell, in his valedictory address as President of the Alpine Club on December 7, 1964, put it well when he said, "My old friend George Mallory's much-quoted remark about climbing Everest 'because it is there' has always given me a shiver down the spine. It doesn't smell of George Mallory one bit. I feel sure that he made it originally as a hurried answer to some boring questioneer (after a lecture, perhaps). He probably meant, 'Don't ask silly questions.' Actually, of course, the reason why any of us want to climb a mountain is because *I am there.*"

What Somervell is saying, of course, is that great things happen when men and mountains meet and that great and strong men are as necessary as great mountains to climbing. Mallory himself, I believe, symbolized this philosophy in his climbing days and spoke meaningfully about the meaning of climbing. It is a piece of writing which may have some relevance to the meaning of our ascent of Everest. I should like to quote it in the context of several paragraphs of David Pye's biographical account of Mallory:

"As a background to this observation and planning of future climbs there was always, as I have said, his preoccupation with the psychological aspect. Almost all his writing about mountains or climbing is coloured by this question of the value of the mountaineer's experience. In the 'Mountaineer as artist' he has given us, vividly enough, his conception of the peculiar quality of mountaineering as an emotional experience. And this was no magazine article written to satisfy the demands of an editor: to Mallory the whole matter of a man's reaction to the mountains was intensely real and important; he returned to it again and again, and even during the war, when the Alps were for years out of reach, it was a subject to which he naturally turned as a refuge.

"When he returned from his season in 1911 it was clear there had been one expedition which stood out for him above all others in this respect. His party had made the traverse of Mont Blanc by the eastern buttress of Mont Maudit. He had been unwell during the earlier part of the climb, and I remember listening as he tried to explain how, gradually, the impressions from without had entered and overcome, bit by bit, the disastrous and defeating emotions which illness and weakness on a mountain produce, till the question of comfort or discomfort ceased to absorb his attention, and he was free, as he said, from himself. In that freedom, moving among some of the noblest sights of the Alps, he learnt something new about the meaning of mountains. He had got hold of some further experience which had affected him powerfully. It is probably impossible to communicate such experiences, though the fact and effect of them may be evident, but to Mallory they were the most important things in mountaineering. He wanted to understand them, to realize their meaning and place in the many-sided whole that

makes up mountaineering experience, and to discover their bearing on the rest of life. It is not a subject which lends itself to precise expression, and he was frankly bothered by the vagueness which seemed unavoidable in any account of it; but this effort to understand became a constant preoccupation with him. Valuing these experiences highly, he desired to be increasingly aware of and responsive to them, and much of his time on mountains and off them was spent in studying the conditions in himself and in others which were most favourable to awareness and to response. The value of an expedition, for him, lay very largely in the extent to which it promoted such experiences, whether by beauty or difficulty or variety or surprise, and in just that measure of freedom, of ready awareness and response, that he found himself. Sometimes the mountains did not do their share, were ugly or repellent, and then he almost hated them. Sometimes he was not able to respond, and then he almost hated himself. 'I was heavy!' he used to say in tones of deep disgust.

"He made an attempt, five years later during idle days in a dugout, to give an account of the Mont Blanc climb seen in retrospect 'from inside, not from outside,' in terms of sensations and emotions rather than of facts. He achieved his end as far, perhaps, as it could be achieved. . . . *'How to get the best of it all? One must conquer, achieve, get to the top; one must know the end to be convinced that one can win the end—to know there's no dream that mustn't be dared. . . . Is this the summit, crowning the day? How cool and quiet! We're not exultant; but delighted, joyful, soberly astonished. . . . Have we vanquished an enemy? None but ourselves. Have we gained success? That word means nothing here. Have we won a kingdom? No . . . and yes. We have achieved an ultimate satisfaction . . . fulfilled a destiny. . . . To struggle and to understand—never this last without the other; such is the law. . . .' "*

The last paragraph of Pye's biography of Mallory has, I think, special meaning for the American expedition to Everest, particularly for the dramatic West Ridge assault, replete as it was with known and unknown dangers:

"When we are tempted to cry out upon the loss of two such lives, it is well for us to try to see Everest as Mallory saw it. To him the attempt was not just an adventure, still less was it an opportunity for record-breaking. The climbing of the mountain was an inspiration because it signified the transcendence of mind over matter. Nowhere as among the high snow and ice is the utter insignificance of man's bodily presence so overwhelming, nowhere as among those mighty masses do his desires and aspirations seem, by comparison, so triumphant. Those two black specks, scarcely visible among the vast eccentricities of nature, but moving up slowly, intelligently, into regions of unknown striving, remain for us a symbol of the invincibility of the human spirit."

—James R. Cox

... the modern mind ... has yielded to the inferior magic of facts, numbers, statistics, and to that sort of empiricism which, in its passion for concreteness, paradoxically reduces experience to a purely abstract notion of measurable data, having cast aside the "immeasurable wealth" of authentic experiences of the spirit and imagination.

—ERIC HELLER

Of all resources the most crucial is Man's spirit.
   Not dulled, nor lulled, supine, secure, replete, does Man create;
   But out of stern challenge, in sharp excitement, with a burning joy;
Man is the hunter still,
   though his quarry be a hope, a mystery, a dream . . .

. . . From what immortal desire, what sudden sight of the unknown,
　　surges that desire?
What flint of fact, what kindling light of art or far horizon,
　　ignites that spark?
What cry, what music, what strange beauty, strikes that resonance?
　　On these hangs the future of the world.

—Nancy Newhall

The first question which you will ask and which I must try to answer is this, "What is the use of climbing Mount Everest?" and my answer must at once be, "It is no use." There is not the slightest prospect of any gain whatsoever. Oh, we may learn a little about the behavior of the human body at high altitudes, where there is only a third of an atmosphere, and possibly medical men may turn our observation to some account for the purposes of aviation. But otherwise nothing will come of it. We shall not bring back a single bit of gold or silver, not a gem, nor any coal or iron. We shall not find a foot of earth that can be planted with crops to raise food. It's no use.

So, if you cannot understand that there is something in man which responds to the challenge of this mountain and goes out to meet it, that the struggle is the struggle of life itself upward and forever upward, then you won't see why we go. What we get from this adventure is just sheer joy. And joy is, after all, the end of life. We do not live to eat and make money. We eat and make money to be able to enjoy life. That is what life means and what life is for.

—George Leigh Mallory

I love the upward ways
To the sun-tipped crest of the mountains
High over the billowy world;
Where the wind sings hymns of praise,
And the snows break into fountains,
And life is a flag unfurled.

—HARRIET MONROE

THE WEST RIDGE

1. Beginnings

IT WAS HOT. Yellow dust rose from beneath our feet, settling opaquely on sunglasses and thickening the sweat on our faces. The warmth of the valley floor at Panchkal was hard to reconcile with February and the ice-sheathed summits thirty miles to the north. The path climbed gently, past open-fronted bazaars and teashops, near the porch of a mud brick house where a woman squatted pounding a large round rock into a mortar filled with rice; beyond, it led through the shade of a corridor of trees, out into the sun again, then up alongside the dry earth of terraced fields awaiting the monsoon. Exertion purged our excesses of soft living and overeating, the first step in the hardening necessary for the weeks ahead, a need my feet were painfully aware of on this second day of our march toward Everest.

Willi Unsoeld and I were far behind the procession, having lingered to say goodbye to Jim Ullman. Panchkal, one day out of Kathmandu, was the end of Jim's journey toward the mountain; the doctors, I among them, had so decreed. The risk to his health, his life, and thus to the prospects of the Expedition was too great. Turning back hadn't been easy—his dream must now walk on without him—and as he wished us a good journey his smile quivered at the edges. There wasn't much to be said, but Willi tried. I stood by awkwardly, impatient to be moving on, not wanting to prolong this farewell. I felt guilty that I was appreciating too little the opportunity to go on toward Everest, an opportunity for which Jim would gladly have sacrificed either leg.

We walked on side by side, following the myriad prints of bare feet in the dust. It was nearly three years since we had known such simple isolation. There was much to be said, once we overcame that feeling of strangeness, wondering how much the other had changed.

"You know, Willi, I'm not very excited about this whole affair. I'm not sure why I came along."

"Me either," he said, "but I've been too swamped to think about it. That's one of the big things I'm looking forward to—just the chance to do some thinking."

"Sometimes I wonder what I hope to get from this trip. For one thing, as far as my own needs go, I don't see how it can touch Masherbrum. This affair is just too big, and people are more diverse. And too much publicity. Still you don't turn down Everest because of that. But if you and Emerson hadn't come, I don't think I would have considered it."

"Guess that's what swung it for me too."

I reminded him of my wife's reaction. Gene had known I would be going back even before I got home from Masherbrum. When she read that I wasn't one of the ones who reached the summit she knew that I still had a question to answer about myself. Apparently she was right, but there was far more to the question than just reaching the top of a mountain. Otherwise why was Willi here? With George Bell, he had made the top of Masherbrum. He had passed the Himalayan test—or had he?

"Not really," he said. "After all, Everest is the ultimate test—in altitude, anyway."

"Well, the way I figure it," I said, "it ought to be a lot easier than Masherbrum, at least by the Col. For one thing there's not nearly the danger we had before, especially from avalanche."

"True, but we're going to hit a lot more wind and cold, and we'll be high a lot longer."

"Sure, but we'll be using oxygen. Physiologically, Everest with oxygen should be easier than Masherbrum without. At least that's what I keep telling myself."

The trail leveled out at the crest of a hill, and aimed at a saddle in the ridge ahead. We started down, leaving the valley of Panchkal behind. A small stream joined us, tumbling temptingly beside the trail in a series of clear pools joined by miniature waterfalls. The melody was too sweet to resist, and we stopped. I sat on the grass, leaning luxuriously against a tree as the chill water anesthetized the raw spots on my heels. Willi poked with a needle from his hat band at a blister engulfing his little toe.

"One thing that bothers me," he said, "is that I've been working so darned hard lately I'm just about run down. I'm exhausted when I climb into bed at night. Maybe the old guide's too far along for this sort of thing."

"Cut it out, old man," I said. "All I hope is you're washed up enough that I can keep up with you."

After a while we pulled on our socks and boots, rose reluctantly, and started up the trail.

Willi resumed, "I guess I'm hunting for some answers too. Where do I go after the Peace Corps? Philosophy, foreign service, or what? That's the big thing I hope this trip will clarify."

"That's asking a lot, Willi—a program for your whole future. But at least you've got some idea of what you're after. I wish I had such a bonafide excuse for being here." I fell silent. Supposedly, my future was all plotted out, at least for the next few years. But something was bugging me. Why was I here? I seemed to be hunting for answers to questions I couldn't even ask. What difference could Everest make even if I got to the top? What was up there to make me any wiser? Nothing but rocks and snow and sky.

There was a time, though, when doubts didn't exist, when the way was unnecessary. Everest was unclimbed. Could it be? Could a man survive at 29,000 feet? That question was a part of me when, at fourteen, I climbed my first mountain in northern Colorado. It was a long gentle walk, rising through a grove of quivering aspen blanketing the crest of an old moraine. I saw the wind-flattened trees at timberline and finally climbed breathlessly over gentle tundra to the summit of Signal Mountain, and tasted the effort of the climb, the soaring freedom waiting at the top. It was a beginning.

Far from the mountains in the winter, I discovered the blurred photo of Everest in Richard Halliburton's *Book of Marvels*. It was a miserable reproduction in which the jagged peaks

rose white against a grotesquely blackened and scratched sky. Everest itself, sitting back from the front ones, didn't even appear the highest, but it didn't matter. It was; the legend said so. Dreams were the key to the picture, permitting a boy to enter it, to stand acrest the high windswept ridge, to climb toward the summit, now no longer far above. My fantasy revealed itself a bit in "Ambition," a theme I wrote in 1946: "I greatly long to someday climb ["another split," exclaimed Margo Johnson, my English teacher] in the Himalayas. I dream of the day when I shall first gaze upon such peaks as Everest, the mysterious Amne Machen, K-2, Kangchenjunga, Nanga Parbat, which has taken so many lives, Nanda Devi, the not quite so high but equally entrancing Mustagh Tower."

This was one of those uninhibited dreams that come free with growing up. I was sure that mine about Everest was not mine alone; the highest point on earth, unattainable, foreign to all experience, was there for many boys and grown men to aspire toward. Even as my love of the mountains grew, and the skill for traveling in them, my dream was buried beneath vocation, marriage, children—a raft of real responsibilities, so full of all the challenge and pleasure a man should ask for that Everest no longer seemed so important.

Anyway it didn't wait. On May 29, 1953, Tenzing and Hillary reached the summit of Everest. Admiration of their achievement mingled with sadness that the struggle was ended, a struggle that now seemed greater in the playing than in the winning. So men could climb it. Had there really ever been any doubt? Did it make man greater or the mountain less? Whatever the answer, the unknown was no longer unknown; a bit more of the dream died.

In the summer of 1960 Nick Clinch invited me to come along to be the climbing doctor for the American-Pakistan Karakoram Expedition to Masherbrum, a beautiful mountain standing icily alone and aloof 25,660 feet high, at the head of the Hushe Valley. The peak had been tried three times before and proved to be properly seasoned with difficulty and danger. We climbed it, and that I failed to reach the summit seemed hardly to matter for I had worked hard; our success was mine, and the depth of companionship would be hard to equal. I had tasted the best there was. The dream of Everest became even less important.

But in May 1961, a postcard came to my home in St. Louis from Norman Dyhrenfurth, saying: "Perhaps you have read that Nepal gave me permission for Everest-Lhotse-Nuptse in 1963? During discussions your name was brought up. If the project interests you, how about mailing me a snapshot, a brief biography and a climbing record? Do let me hear from you."

Everest. The old distant longings stirred. It might be fun, I thought, especially if George Bell and Dick Emerson and Willi Unsoeld were to go. I didn't need to go, for Masherbrum had quenched my thirst. But a chance just to see the highest point on earth? I doubted that the money could ever be raised. But I might as well say I was interested and see what developed.

On May 13 I replied: "Yes, the project 'interests' me considerably. It is too soon to be sure of availability, though I would guess the chances are excellent.

"Incidentally, I have been fiddling with one of the Swiss oxygen masks in the lab and believe it can be improved to perform much more efficiently. If you're interested, I shall be happy to give you details when the tests are completed."

This brought an airmail letter in response: "Your letter of May 13, was welcome news, indeed. We have decided on a total of fifteen men, fourteen of whom are able to go 'high.'

"As to the question of oxygen, I agree that the equipment could stand some improvements. If it is O.K. with you, I would like to put you in charge of oxygen equipment from here on in."

During the next eighteen months the Expedition ripened to solvent reality under Norman's imaginative guidance. On February 3, 1963, we were on our way. I sat, seat belt fastened, heavy with an emptiness, and began a letter to my wife, who stood a hundred yards away inside the terminal.

My pen paused as loneliness and doubt overwhelmed me. I wanted to get off the plane and walk those hundred yards and forget this nonsense. But I couldn't—and live with myself. As suddenly as it had welled up, the feeling subsided, but the pain lingered, perhaps to intensify by contrast the pleasure I knew would come. Parting from Gene, I felt the bond of years tug stronger than it ever had before; paradoxically, the feeling diminished loneliness.

A restless urge to come to grips with the mountain, and myself, pulled me on. After three years of civilized living I needed proof of my ability to tolerate such an environment once again, and I needed time for introspection to try to understand an urge that mixed so much sadness with expectancy. I felt strangely assured that I would get to the top. This arose from something intangible, beyond just prior knowledge of what Everest was like. But looked at objectively, clearly, my confidence was irrational. Weather could effect the success of the entire undertaking; my own health and performance at 32 might turn out poor compared to what it was in 1960; I might not be in the right place at the right time; and there were eighteen others, of impressive stature physically and presumably of equal motivation. All these reasons made my hopes unrealistic, but the dream was fully alive now and it wouldn't let go.

2. Gestation

THE SECOND night we camped at Dolalghat, on the point of land separating the Sun Kosi and Indrawati Kosi. The confluence of these two large rivers marked the low point in our journey, not quite two thousand feet above sea level. Dick, Willi, and I spent the afternoon at the river, washing a few clothes, watching two giggling Sherpanis who flirtingly bathed just above us, then wandered off downstream. After a few gasps when we took the first cold plunge, we found the water pleasantly tolerable. We played like boys suddenly freed from school for the summer, inventing games, seeking challenges. Wading into the current we crossed the painfully rocky bottom to the other side, hobbled upstream, and floated back across to our landing. Then, discovering a wonderful selection of flat, smooth stones, we began skipping them along the surface of the water, seeing how much mileage we could put into each spinning disk. Willi finally sent one skittering out onto the opposite river bank, providing a new challenge for Dick and me. I succeeded once in delivering a stone to the other side; Willi and Dick possessing more skill, power, and wrist dexterity, soon attained enviable regularity.

A lean, young porter stopped on the opposite shore to watch, fascinated. He tried to throw the stones back, at first awkwardly, as he attempted to mimic Unsoeld's style, but soon he was accurately skipping them onto our beach. Once he and Willi managed to exchange the same stone twice without wetting its upper side. After a time he waved thanks for the new-found game and wandered downstream.

As in this game, communication between Sahib and Sherpa was largely unspoken; few of our Sherpas knew much English and we were even worse off. Jimmy Roberts, or Noddy, or even Gombu could bridge the gap for us when they were around, and old Tashi, who had been with Tilman on Everest in 1938, had an impressive vocabulary. If there was reason behind Tashi's choice of words, there wasn't any in the order of their arrangement. They came forth scrambled, challenging the listener to sort them out and reassemble them in a sensible sequence. Whether we understood Tashi is something we were never quite sure of. In spite of this linguistic limitation, or because of it, communication with our Sherpas at a deeper level never was a problem.

The people living in the Solu Khumbu, the high hills around the base of Everest, were, like the hills themselves, unencumbered by civilization and were full of fun. Some, infected with Western man's ailments, were opportunists, like our sirdar, Pasang Phutar. A few were lazy, though rarely so skillfully as the doctor's dapper helper, Angayle. Most of them were willing to work hard, in part because that was what they were paid for, and in part out of respect for the men with whom they climbed. They were shrewd judges of character, and they sought it inside the man.

As for me, the novelty never quite wore off of coming into camp each afternoon to find a smiling Tenzing Nindra waiting to remove my pack. As I settled luxuriously into a chair, he returned with camp shoes to replace the blister pounders I had been wearing during the day. Sitting relaxed in the warm afternoon, a can of beer in one hand, I remembered the *San Francisco Chronicle* headline on our day of departure about "The New Soft Life on Mt. Everest." When I headed for the sack at night, there was my whole bed laid out, blown up, fluffed, with pajamas laid neatly on top. Our first reaction back in the States was that this might be all right for the British or Swiss, but independent American types could never tolerate being waited upon. Now, all I wondered was whether I'd remember how to blow up my air mattress at twenty-six thousand feet when Tenzing wasn't available. This ritual was an ingrained part of the relationship, easier to accept than to change, or so we rationalized. I suspect it was not a chore for our Sherpas and there was no hint of servitude. I wondered whether their solicitousness was not designed to spare their frail Sahibs' limited energy for the effort ahead.

* * *

From Dolalghat, we climbed steeply to make camp on the open slopes of the ridge at Chaubas, five thousand feet higher. It was a hot day and the occasional shade of banyan trees planted for rest stops came as a thankful oasis. At camp that evening we gathered in the large tent to discuss our mountaineering goal—climbing of the three peaks enclosing the Western Cwm. All had been climbed before: Everest in 1953, and again in 1956; Lhotse, by the 1956 Swiss expedition; and Nuptse, from the other side by the British in 1961. It remained for us to climb all three, to achieve a grand slam unique in the history of Himalayan mountaineering. Since Norman had capitalized on this in his tireless search for funds, we had an obligation to it. But who among us would rather climb Lhotse than Everest? Or the long, many-summited ridge of Nuptse? Somehow, to a group of mountaineers, the prospect of these re-ascents lacked challenge. There was a way out: a new route on Everest.

I had first heard about it when Norman came to visit in San Diego. Photos were unfurled and laid end to end across our living room floor to make a vast panorama—held in place by children's blocks. While I looked at our triple goal, Norm asked, with a matter-of-factness that seemed irreverent to the highest mountain on earth, "What do you think of trying the West Ridge? Maybe it wouldn't be so bad if we went up from the South Col and then descended to a camp at 25,000 feet." The idea of a new route sounded wild to me. Wasn't it enough to climb by the regular way?

But Norm had planted the idea and a boyhood dream was alive again: Everest, and by a new route. I kept the dream vivid with a copy of the 1954 *Mountain World* that lay for weeks upon my desk, open to an Indian Air Force photo of Everest from the west. With greater and greater ease, I escaped in the course of those weeks to the black snow-etched rock of the West

Ridge. That slope looks O.K. if we can get out of the Cwm to it—maybe across those slabs, and up that thin gully of snow. I wonder if it goes clear through those cliffs at 28,000. If only I could see into that gully. Looks steep though. Can't tell from the picture. Still, it might be a way. But don't be ridiculous, Tom. That's Everest you're looking at.

At our shake-down cruise on Mount Rainier in the fall of 1962 Norm said: "Let's not let our thoughts leak out to the press. We can talk more about the West Ridge when we're on the way." But many of us couldn't wait.

"What do you think of Norm's idea the other night of descending the West Ridge?" Barry Corbet asked.

"Sounds great if he wants to do it," I replied. "But no thanks; I'm too chicken. Can you imagine yourself dragging over the summit of Everest from the Col side, running on the dregs of your oxygen, and then plunging down an unknown route? With a camp waiting four thousand feet below? Hell, if you get into trouble three hundred feet down, you've had it. You could never get back up over the top."

Barry asked, "Then why not move the camp up closer to the top?"

"Sure," Dick Emerson agreed. "In that case you might as well go *up* the ridge. It'd be just as easy, and a heck of a lot safer."

"Well, Norm was trying to do it without plowing too much effort into that side," I said, remembering that he felt it would take less equipment to go down it than to go up.

"Still, it sounds like suicide to me," Dick said.

"Maybe we can make a double traverse," Jake Breitenbach suggested. "One team up each side, trade a man at the top, and then descend both routes."

"How are you going to decide which pair goes down which way?"

"They can fight it out."

Barry Bishop was struck by the casualness with which we toyed with the idea.

"Delusions of grandeur," he had said.

* * *

Now, at Chaubas, was a good time to look at the delusions as a group. What about the West Ridge? Its appeal was tremendous, but how could it fit into our plan for the Grand Slam?

"The West Ridge will be a hell of a lot more impressive if we can pull it off," Dan Doody said.

"But if we don't pull it off, we might end up with nothing," Norm replied.

"To the mountaineering world, even a good attempt would be a significant achievement," Dick Emerson said.

But there were many other things to weigh, not all of them mountaineering considerations. Norm pointed out, "This may sound like Madison Avenue kind of talk, but you know how long it took to raise our money and, I repeat, the Swiss have done Everest and Lhotse. If we do less than that as an expedition, to the world, not to mountaineers, we are less successful."

Bishop thought that the photographic possibilities on the West Ridge would be spectacular. It was his opinion that the National Geographic Society would be enthusiastic about a West Ridge attempt, and after all, they were our largest single contributor.

Since we were discussing all the possibilities, we might as well be thorough, I thought. Besides, a good trader always asks more than he expects to get. I suggested "Why not just dump the Col Route and put the entire expedition on the West Ridge? This would give us the best possible chance of climbing it."

There was a brief silence as the import of my suggestion sank in, then vigorous rebuttal, underlain, I suspected, with unspoken doubt about Hornbein's judgment, if not his sanity. This single remark was to have a lasting effect, typing me as an outspoken advocate of the West Ridge route.

Norman set forth his own reactions in his diary: ". . . we talked very frankly about the thing that had been on the minds of all the climbers: the West Ridge. If we can pull it off it would be the biggest possible thing still to be accomplished in Himalayan mountaineering. It was interesting to see how highly motivated the whole group was. There was comparatively little interest in Lhotse and Nuptse although I had explained to them that initially, when we were trying to raise funds, the idea of an American 'Grand Slam' of the three peaks had its appeal. But to most of the men that meant very little. In fact, Tom Hornbein, who is such an idealist and so enthusiastic about the West Ridge, declared himself in favor of throwing everything into that attempt, even if it meant jeopardizing success altogether. At this point I had to speak up strongly. I'm all for making a serious stab at the West Ridge—a thorough reconnaissance to see if it's feasible—and then pushing a line of camps up it, but at the same time establishing camps along the old route. Then possibly we can have the main attempt by the West Ridge, but must still be sure, as a back up, to have a four-man attempt, with support, from the South Col. Only this way can we be certain of success—or at least as certain as one can be on a mountain like Everest. Everyone agreed with that point of view. We have —almost *have*—to have a success. If later on we say, 'We tried the more difficult route of the West Ridge and bogged down,' that will be a very lame excuse for all the people who backed us. So we will try both."

Our discussion at Chaubas fixed the Ridge firmly in many minds. The days passed by in rapid succession, each vanishing into the vat of yesterdays. Past events took on a fuzzy reality. Letting my diary lapse for one evening, the next night I was faced with the problem: "It is startling how hazy yesterday's march has become. As a matter of fact, it is—ah yes, here it comes. At 6:30 after tea I started out with the front runners— Dick Pownall, Lute Jerstad, Bishop, and Breitenbach—enjoying the view as we traversed the ridge. We breakfasted a little after nine, then we dropped through beautiful pine forests, a long way down. Seduced by the crystalline clarity of a flowing stream, we picked a particularly delectable pool, stripped, soaked, and then dove. Was it ice! But tingling, invigorating, and so lasting that I scarcely sweated the last hour of the uphill journey."

Heat and dust, and the realization that soon all the water we saw would be in the form of snow and ice, convertible to liquid only by patient melting over a butane stove, caused us

to cherish these interludes. Sometimes Willi and I, far back from the rest, would wander from the path to find a particularly delightful pool. Other times, most of the team would join the game, some shedding shirts to air and sun themselves while others stripped for the icy plunge. The temperature of the water offered a Spartan challenge; the first touch of a toe convinced you you didn't need a bath at all and anyway, evaporation of a sweat-soaked T-shirt was cooling enough. But the sun was warm and the pool was inviting, so you soap all over to insure against faintness of heart. Now committed, you take the plunge and gasp until your skin is numb.

There were many such baths, and soon we became spoiled when a day went by without one. One day, Dave Dingman, Willi, Jake, and I enjoyed the added pleasure of running the rapids. The water, not too cold for a change, coursed down narrow channels through a series of large bathtubs, finally emptying into a calm pool edged by a sandy beach. Diving from a boulder fifty yards upstream, we were carried down by the current. Flowing with the water, we alternately bent and arched to avoid scraping our undercarriage on the rocks beneath but still ended up with slightly sandpapered chest and thighs as the price of our wild refreshing ride. Most people preferred it as a spectator sport.

The one evil of these interludes was that it took fortitude to dress and move on again, slipping into rusksacks that were now putting callouses on the grooves carved in our shoulders. By jamming my black umbrella into the ski slot of my pack, I could hike in the shade, occasionally even catching the hint of a breeze.

Once there were tangerines, five for half a Nepalese rupee, deliciously sweet but tantalizingly scarce. Mostly, we put in hours of conversation, while strolling downhill, or sitting under banyan trees watching the line of porters and children passing. Sometimes, we pumped Dick for clues to his sociological study and the purpose of the diaries we filled in each evening. His replies were put in the frustrating language of his profession, designed not only to be truthful but also to be completely unenlightening. Invariably, we returned to the West Ridge, planning, weighing, examining our own and each other's goals.

The question, as Dave put it one night, was who would be willing to pour his energy into the West Ridge, with failure as a not unlikely outcome, when reaching the summit by the South Col seemed so much more assured.

"I can see a situation," he said, "where you might be forerunners on the West Ridge and only get to 24,000 while other people are going back and forth to the summit on the other route."

"I'm not sure I like the alternative you pose, Dave," Dick said. "I'd like to *go to* the summit via the West Ridge."

"I don't think anyone wants to try the West Ridge route and work on it," Barry Corbet added, "unless there is *some* possibility of getting to the summit."

I agreed with Barry, but that word "some" was troublesome. How much gamble was a person willing to take? How much of a shoestring would he be willing to go on? Dick, Willi, and I had devoted a good portion of one day's stroll to trying to handle this question. Dick had suggested that even an attentuated re-

connaissance of the West Ridge might be worth the effort if there were hope of "lucking out" and reaching the summit. To me, the less we depended on luck, the better. In the end all three of us agreed that as long as there was any chance of success we'd stay with the West Ridge.

"The reason I asked the question," Dave continued, "was that the guys that go up and beat away at the West Ridge aren't going to be in any shape to climb anything else. They aren't going to go up and work for three weeks on the West Ridge and then come down and go up the Col."

Dick agreed: "If you go to work on the West Ridge, you realize that that's your part of the expedition."

Dan Doody felt we were all wasting our time talking, since Dave's question really couldn't be answered until a reconnaissance had been made.

Before we had even come within sight of the mountain, most of us had done battle with Dave's question and reached at least a tentative decision. Some preferred to sink their efforts into the Col route; some were confirmed West Ridgers, verging on the obnoxious in their enthusiasm; and a few maintained a Col-leaning neutrality, dictated by scientific obligations or a genuine desire to go where most needed.

On the surface, the choice seemed to be based on climbing interests and skills: rock scramblers on the West Ridge, iceclimbers on the Col route. Underneath lurked far more important intangibles; similarities or fine differences in philosophies, moral values, social interests. Curiously, with the exception of Willi, not one of the Ridgers had ever engaged in competitive sports; most of the South Colers had. What really lay at the root of each man's answer to Dave's question was another question, one for our psychologist, Jim Lester, to try to answer. But he never answered questions; he only asked them.

* * *

For those who didn't dally, our daily treks ended early in the afternoon, but rarely before the heat and aching feet forced us to ask each passing Sherpa, "How much farther to camp?" The reply, we soon were to discover, was invariable: "Only two mile more, Sah'b." Still, we never ceased asking and only rarely were we disappointed with the reply.

Afternoons we spent relaxing; watching the younger generation climbing banyan trees, secretly hoping that the "Great Equalizer," altitude, would even things out once we were on the mountain; observing Jim Whittaker polishing off his daily five dozen push-ups; grimacing from the pain of squeezing Pownall's grip-tester; or just sitting, clutching a can of beer, looking at clouds and dreaming. On days when stops for chang (a beverage made from fermented rice) were too abundant we often arrived before our porters. Then we would sit up on the hillside waiting for them. Sculpting moleskin pads for blisters took an hour or so, especially for Willi's, outshone only by the horrors on the bottoms of Jim Lester's feet.

There were other constructive moments in these afternoons. Dick and I, sometimes with Willi or Barry Bishop or others, retreated to a quiet tent to calculate equipment and personnel needs of the Expedition. Dick had laid the groundwork for these logistics back in the States. Attacking a mountain of de-

tails, he gave shape, with his analytical mind, to the final scheme: start with what's needed for the final day at the highest camp, then work down an ever-enlarging pyramid of supply. How much goes above Camp 5 and what's used there? Add them together. That's what we have to carry above Camp 4. And so on down the mountainside.

"For two man teams, how much oxygen do we need at 6?"

"Two bottles per man to the summit. That'd be eight bottles for two assaults plus one per pair per night for sleep. How many nights should we figure?"

"We have got to keep it thin for the carries. Let's say three, total. That gives one team a possibility of an extra night in case of bad weather, or if they're late coming down."

"Well, that's eight bottles for climbing, three sleep, eleven bottles in all. Times thirteen, what's that . . .?"

"A hundred and forty-three pounds."

"Ugh! O.K. One two-man tent, that's twelve pounds, the Sahibs can carry their own personal gear and air mattresses, and sleeping bags. Now, food?"

"Better stretch that a little farther than the oxygen, in case someone gets pinned down by a storm up there. How about six days?"

"No, that's forty pounds. Four days ought to be enough. Once the oxygen's gone they'll have to come down anyway."

"O.K. Butane? The three pounders are good for nine hours each."

"Two enough?"

"Don't forget a cook pot." Unsoeld said, recalling the day on Masherbrum when he was forced to cook in a hastily emptied tuna can because I forget to send utensils.

"That adds up to 215 pounds. With six carries, that's about thirty-five pounds per man, not counting the bottle they use to climb."

"That's way too much for 27,000 feet," Willi said.

"Yes, but using oxygen they'll only be nineteen thousand inside their mask." I replied.

"Maybe so," Willi said. "But that's still a hell of a load."

"My God! We haven't figured any oxygen for a traverse team if they come down by the Col. What are we going to do about that?" Dick asked.

"Let 'em rough it." Willi suggested.

"Well, maybe we can get the high carry to leave their half-empty bottles at 6 and go down to the Col without oxygen." I suggested.

And so the calculations went, fattening exponentially downward, till all the combinations were computed, digested, summarized, and typed out for presentation to the team.

Evenings were peaceful, smoke settling in the quiet air to soften the dusk, lights twinkling on the ridge we would camp on tomorrow, clouds dimming the outline of our pass for the day after. Growing excitement lured my thoughts again and again to the West Ridge. My dreams were of the reconnaissance of the West Shoulder and the possibilities that lay above. I hoped I would be a part of it.

There was loneliness, too, as the sun set, but only rarely now did doubts return. Then I felt sinkingly as if my whole life lay behind me. Once on the mountain I knew (or trusted) that this would give way to total absorption with the task at hand. But at times I wondered if I had not come a long way only to find that what I really sought was something I had left behind.

Narrative continues on page 58

Something hidden. Go and find it.
Go and look behind the Ranges—
Something lost behind the Ranges.
Lost and waiting for you. Go!
—KIPLING

What a wonderful voyage through time and space!

After having flown over the plains of India, flat as the sea, we were crossing Nepal on foot and approaching at last the highest mountains on earth.

One evening the deep narrow valley suddenly fanned out, and the dream that we had nursed for so many long years began to take shape. Far up, between the lilac mists that concealed the foot of the gigantic mountain and the raw blue of the Asian sky, floated a tracery of stone at more than twenty-six thousand feet; slopes of snow, torn by the wind, evaporated into azure . . .

Silently we advanced a little, leaving behind us the tumult of the torrent buffeting through its gorges. In the stillness that followed we could hear better the murmurings of nature and the beating of our own hearts. For a long time we gazed at the mysterious mountain which had enchanted our evenings around the camp-fire; then, when my eyes could look away along the immense valley bottom, utterly silent and deserted, I thought of the Oisans, of the Valais, of the Oberland, and I said to myself: "This place is just like home, only on a larger scale! It is one of those places marked in ochre and white in the atlas, high, sterile and good for nothing; nothing marketable grows there, and higher still nothing can exist at all. It is one of those spots made solely for the happiness of men, in order that in this changing world, grown every day more artificial, they might yet find a few gardens still unspoiled in their silence of forgetfulness, a few gardens full of primal colours that are good for the eyes and for the heart."

That evening, when the sun dipped behind the earth, I experienced a deep feeling of serenity in the presence of so many natural things: the wood fire, the valley which drew us on, the magnetic mountains, the air of peace and silence, the living sky. I was happy to be there; and, thinking of my boyhood, of my very first excursion in the mountains, so like the one we were making now, I said to myself again: "It's just like the first time."
—GASTON REBUFFAT

RICHARD M. EMERSON: Distant houses and high ranges, from near Gauri Sankar

RICHARD M. EMERSON: Houses near Sete
THOMAS HORNBEIN: On the approach

Mountains are the beginning and the end of all natural scenery.

—John Ruskin

Men go to the mountains because they need the mountains—because they find behind the ranges things that are hidden from them in the life of the plains. "Our present world," the distinguished climber, Frederic Harrison, once said, "is a world of remarkable civilization, but it is not very natural and not very happy. We need some snatches of the life of youth—to be for a season simply happy and simply healthy. We need sometimes that poetry should not be droned into our ears, but flashed into our senses. And, man, with all his knowledge and his pride, needs sometimes to know nothing and to feel nothing, but that he is a marvellous atom in a marvellous world."

There has been no time in human history when mountains and mountaineering have had so much to offer to men. We need to re-discover the vast, harmonious pattern of the natural world we are a part of—the infinite complexity and variety of its myriad components, the miraculous simplicity of the whole. We need to learn again those essential qualities in our own selves which make us what we are: the energy of our bodies, the alertness of our minds; curiosity and the desire to satisfy it, fear and the will to conquer it. The mountain way may well be a way of escape—from the cities and men, from the turmoil and doubt, from the perplexities and uncertainties and sorrows that thread our lives. But in the truest and most profound sense it is an escape not *from* but *to* reality.

—James R. Ullman

The mountains can be reached in all seasons. They offer a fighting challenge to heart, soul and mind, both in summer and winter. If throughout time the youth of the nation accept the challenge the mountains offer, they will help keep alive in our people the spirit of adventure. That spirit is a measure of the vitality of both nations and men. A people who climb the ridges and sleep under the stars in high mountain meadows, who enter the forest and scale peaks, who explore glaciers and walk ridges buried deep in snow—these people will give their country some of the indomitable spirit of the mountains.

—Wm O. Douglas

I say that the qualities which strike every sensitive observer are impressed upon the mountaineer with tenfold force and intensity. . . . He has learnt a language which is but partially revealed to ordinary men. An artist is superior to an unlearned picture-seer, not merely because he has greater natural sensibility, but because he has improved it by methodical experience; because his senses have been sharpened by constant practice, till he can catch finer shades of colouring, and more delicate inflexions of line; because, also, the lines and colours have acquired new significance, and been associated with a thousand thoughts with which the mass of mankind has never cared to connect them. The mountaineer is improved by a similar process.

—Sir Leslie Stephen

To those who have struggled with them the mountains reveal beauties they will not disclose to those who make no effort. That is the reward the mountains give to effort. And it is because they have so much to give and give it so lavishly to those who will wrestle with them that men love the mountains and go back to them again and again . . . the mountains reserve their choice gifts for those who stand upon their summits.

—SIR FRANCIS YOUNGHUSBAND

This thought alone stood out clearly in my mind during that first period of repose, after the great excitement my senses had undergone; my muscles were still shaking with the efforts they had put forth; as I lay motionless on a rock I still had a feeling of continued motion, as when one disembarks after a stormy passage. And yet I discovered within me an exceptional mental balance, a security, a strange keenness in all my faculties, as if the content had awakened hitherto unsuspected powers in me. I enjoyed the repose like a healthy animal that comes weary but victorious out of a fight, sure of its strength and its cunning and ready to fight again.

It may be that this suddenly revived consciousness of inherited instinctive faculties is one of the deepest and most acceptable self-revelations which we attain through the savage struggle with the mountains, and it is each time a cause of surprise, and almost a shock to us, as if a being new and unknown had made his appearance in us, and for the time replaced that other individual, full of weaknesses and pride, who is wont to walk in our likeness during our daily life in cities.

It seems as if the modern, civilized man, sated with artificialities and luxury, were wont, when he returns to the primeval mountains, to find among their caves his prehistoric brother, alive and unchanged, a simple child of Nature, whose foot is sure and whose eye is accustomed to wide spaces; he seems to recognize with joy a survivor of his family's early unrecorded struggles with untamed Nature, to unite with him, and to let himself be led through the terrible visions of a prehistoric landscape, to renew for a day the ancient war which tempered the human race in its infancy.

—GUIDO REY

And this, our life, exempt from public haunt, finds tongues in trees, books in the running brooks, sermons in stones, and good in everything.

—SHAKESPEARE

The little family of plants lives on this lofty spot, far from its peers, rooted in the sparse soil, watered by the rain showers, content with the bright sunshine and the friendly shade of the clouds. It lives the same humble, vigorous life that we seek in the mountains; those brave, gay flowers expressed to me in the vigorous language of their beautiful colours their joy in living. They are symbols of Nature's victorious force against every obstacle, but they spoke to me of the wholesomeness of struggle, of faith in the usefulness of life, and they repeated to me the true words of the Sermon on the Mount: "Considerate lilia quomodo crescunt. . . ."

—GUIDO REY

These pools that, though in forests, still reflect
The total sky almost without defect,
    And like the flowers beside them, chill and shiver,
Will like the flowers beside them soon be gone,
    And yet not out by any brook or river,
But up by roots to bring dark foliage on.

The trees that have it in their pent-up buds
To darken nature and be summer woods—
    Let them think twice before they use their powers
To blot out and drink up and sweep away
    These flowery waters and these watery flowers
From snow that melted only yesterday.

                    —ROBERT FROST

Beside the lane up which we used to pass every day as children stood a school, with a belfry. The belfry was glazed with small panes of amethyst-coloured glass. Into and out of this floating sky-palace the folk of Fairyland flitted and sang. It was the playground for all the realities of a childs' dream world. When I walk under it now, I see a vane and a box of pink glass, with some darker ruby panes, ill-matched but not unpleasing; they seem to blush for their past frailty, for the brittle charms that tempted and fell before the mischievous gravel from the boys' yard. The fairies, with the light just catching the underside of their wings as they hovered across the pink sills, are all gone. But I can never pass the belfry without a catch of the breath, an involuntary hushing of the step. Something has all but happened, or is all but going to happen when I have passed. The fairies are waiting, only anxious to be again discovered; it is I who have moved off a little, and can no longer quite see them.

Mountains may have something of the same message, even for our later life. At night, especially, they seem to be waiting breathlessly, full of a rushing silence of unseen presences and of a wondering curiosity as to whether we shall hear or see "this time." At moments when we are alone or when we have in imagination "put out a little from the land," we can almost *feel* their secret. But with the effort to shape it into words its meaning escapes us, like the music we have heard in dreams; or it becomes commonplace, like a drying sea-pebble from which the beauty passes with the shadow of its moisture.

                  —GOEFFREY WINTHROP YOUNG

3. Wilderness

EACH DAY was a small world, complete, sufficient unto itself. I jealously cherished the hours of walking, of sitting in the shade, of sharing hopes, of exploring the near beauty and the far. All was pure pleasure; not even growing enthusiasm for the West Ridge could detract from it. Thoughts of the approaching effort seemed to heighten the peace of the march. The time to push would come soon enough.

As we traveled eastward across the grain of the country, blisters healed, muscles hardened, and even the sunburnt red of my balding brow took on a pain-free tan. There was rarely a chance for us to become bored with the terrain. From Yersa we dropped steeply 2,000 feet to the Bhote Kosi, crossed a chain bridge, then climbed about 5,000 feet up the other side. The first half was quite steep—not much fiddling around with switchbacks in this country—but in the early morning shade it proved enjoyable. The rest, beneath the blistering sun, was fortunately more gradual, past terraced fields extending for thousands of feet above and below us.

At the pass a few deep red rhododendrons bloomed, and small white orchids grew in the gnarled bark of some pin oaks. The distant view was breathtaking enough to be hard on constantly stubbed toes. Ridges and valleys meshed to the north of us like fingers intertwined, each separated by steadily deepening purple haze. Shimmering ice-white in the morning sun, Gaurisanker and Menlungste rose like gigantic teeth, separating purple hills from a deep blue sky. With binoculars we would follow the white rampart eastward over nameless peaks, searching. Always the object of our search was concealed behind the nearer ranges.

Our daily ups and downs did not quite balance. The farther east we traveled, the higher and more immense the country became until on the eleventh day we crossed into a different world. Our predawn starts had been growing colder, and on this particular morning a light drizzle added to our shivering as we began our climb to 12,500 feet, our highest pass. An hour brought us to the monastery; another hour of gradual climb along the ridge to breakfast. Barry Corbet was at low ebb, pale and unstable after a bout of diarrhea, but he plodded gamely through the long day. Morning sun, streaming toward us through tall firs, brilliantly backlit the snow-dusted needles. We passed some zhos being milked. As the day wore on the clouds closed in on us.

Behind as usual, Willi and I strolled alone through a silent forest of gnarled, moss-hung rhododendron trees. In place of leaves, snow clung to the skyward edge of each branch. The thin winding track through the snow was stained brown by the passing of feet, some bare, impervious to cold. Fog wreathed the trees, subduing the winter color of the forest to black and white and gray. Existence began and ended here, enclosed by a mist that captured sound and concealed the view. None of the vastness outside seeped in.

Then the forest was gone and we were in high open tundra.

Clusters of bamboo poles anchored by mounds of piled rocks marked the pass. The prayer flags at their tops would have flapped in the wind but a crust of rime immobilized them. We paused for a moment, then plunged down the other side, descending through open forests of tall firs, through a narrow wooded valley with a tumbling mountain stream on its floor, finally coming out on the high edge of a new country. Terraces were gone, instead rolling meadows had been cleared from the forest. Stands of fir and pine looked like cloud shadows on the hillsides. A stream wound silver along the valley floor. A few zhos and horses grazed beside green fields of spring-ripening wheat. Beside the trail strawberry plants were flowering and our mouths watered in anticipation. A cluster of well-ordered houses climbed the hill above the stream. Willi and I walked down the wide path toward the village, feeling that we had been here before.

From the beginning we had seen virtually no wilderness. Rice terraces had climbed thousands of feet up hillsides, prayer flags flapped at the passes; paths occasionally edged with mani walls crisscrossed the country. For all the size, for all the intransigent power of the ice-encrusted wall to the north, wilderness, as western man defines it, did not exist. Yet there was no impression of nature tamed. It seemed to me that here man lived in continuous harmony with the land, as much and as briefly a part of it as all its other occupants. He used the earth with gratitude, knowing that care was required for continued sustenance. He rotated crops, controlled the cutting of wood, bulwarked his fields against erosion. In this peaceful co-existence, man was the invited guest. It was an enviable symbiosis. The Expedition surely must have affected this balance: a thousand porters living off the produce of the land, a mixing of peoples, the economic stresses, the physical impact itself. Although we touched each place for only a day and then moved on, I wondered how many such passings could be made before the imprint would become indelible. But awareness of our effect on the land was lost beneath the effect of the land and its people on us. At each day's camp we watched curiously villagers curiously watching us. In the evenings we often escaped to the future, planning.

One evening we presented our calculations to the team, and there were plenty of questions. Everyone explored the possible combinations of two-man summit-assault teams by the West Ridge with two, four, or six by the Col. Only the six-man Col team was clearly incompatible with a West Ridge attempt. Our calculations showed that two-man West Ridge teams required the same number of carries as four-man teams on the other route.

"Why is that?" Lute asked.

"The Dump we're figuring on the West Ridge essentially amounts to an extra camp," Dick replied.

When the suggestion was made to split the carrying power equally between the two routes, Norman voiced his concern.

"I'd like to give a word of warning. Let's not go overboard on the West Ridge. I am just as excited about the West Ridge as you are. I've thought about it, I think, a good deal longer than most of you. But let's not jeopardize the South Col. Let's not make the mistake of throwing all the power, all the oxygen, into the West Ridge, because the Col is still our guarantee of success."

"This brings up the question," I said, "of the size of the South Col party, assuming the West Ridge is going to be tried. It's been debatable between two- and four-man teams. I know there are different impressions about where we stand on this."

"Tom, I don't think we can make the final plan yet." Norm said, "Everybody has to be at Advance Base."

"I agree," I replied, "but if you want to succeed in climbing both routes, the chances are increased by not having a four-man assault on the South Col. Putting two-man teams up the South Col permits a stronger effort on the West Ridge and also increases your chance of success on the South Col."

Gil Roberts reasoned differently: "Given four men in Camp 6 as opposed to two men, I think you've got a better chance of making the summit. If you have only a two-man team and one of them craps out, that shoots your whole attempt."

Gil's statement was true as far as it went. But weather was less dependable than health. If you put all your hopes on a four-man team and had a bad day all four would be shot down. It would be better to send up teams on successive days, and it would require half as much equipment and manpower for two-man teams as for four-man teams. This was my reasoning and Will Siri agreed.

Norm was puzzled. "Somehow this doesn't look right," he said. "I mean there have been several expeditions that have been uniquely successful with large summit teams. Dhaulagiri is one, Jannu is one, Makalu is—there are arguments on both sides."

Will answered, "Yes, but these have all been peaks that are substantially lower than Mount Everest."

"Dhaulagiri isn't, without oxygen," Norm observed; "that makes it just as high."

I considered the number of carries required just to move our ton of oxygen bottles to the upper slopes of Everest, and answered, "No it doesn't, Norman. Logistically it makes Dhaulagiri a hell of a lot easier."

"Let me inject one thing here," Will said. "I think everyone is aware of the enthusiasm that permeates the whole group, the drives and everything else. The ultimate decision, let's face it,

has to rest with Norman. He's been here before. He knows the problems and he can see the overall picture; and furthermore, neither Norman or I are motivated by the desire to get to the summit of the peak. Neither of us entertains any hopes of getting to the summit. Maybe to the South Col, yes, possibly; but I think this gives Norman a little more objectivity than the rest of us, plus a vast amount of experience which the rest of us don't possess, and I think you're going to have to go along with him on certain items, certain concepts here."

"Unspoken consensus on that point, Will," Dick said.

Will continued: "I think we should agree at the outset on this. Each of us has his own drives, motives, and inclinations in this no matter how objective we try to be. This is going to influence our thinking. Furthermore, this Expedition as an organization has certain overriding obligations. The mountaineering one is to get to the summit of Everest. The most obvious route, or the route with the highest probability at the moment, is certainly the South Col. If it gives us a higher measure of assurance of success so far as the Expedition is concerned, then this has got to be pushed through."

"Yes," Jim Whittaker said, "we all agree on the fact, Will. We must reach the summit. That's the utmost in our minds and all of us agree that the South Col is the obvious route. There is no question of that in our minds."

"As long as that is clear," Norm said.

Jim replied. "That is clear. We know we have to get the mountain."

"Yes," Dick added, "All of us understand that the West Ridge is just frosting on the cake and nothing more."

As Willi seconded Dick's statement, I sat silently thinking I much preferred frosting, and Jim said; "Norman, I think as long as we can have these talks like this and we can align our thoughts so that we can know that your desire is to do exactly what we're trying to do—I mean as long as we feel, or as long as you feel, we're not sacrificing anything on the South Col for this and that, I think that we'll be able to move ahead in the right direction."

"I think you know me well enough by now," Norm replied, "to know that I am not a dictator, never will be." There were nods of agreement. "But there are some basic things I will have to insist on."

"Right," Jim said. "That's fine as long as you let us know, so we don't go off half-cocked."

4. Bouldering

ON THE third of March we crossed our final pass, the Taksindu Banyang, at 10,000 feet. Throughout our eastward journey the country had grown in vastness and depth. Here the bottom seemed to drop out and a whole complex of ridges and hillsides fell toward the silent thread of river a mile below. "That's the Dudh Kosi, the Milky River," Norm said. "We'll cross it tomorrow." His face showed his pleasure in having once again, after several years, come home. This was the place he knew, the Solu Khumbu, the home of the Sherpas. That moving thin line of white so far below was a raging torrent, the largest we would have to cross. It was no harder to believe that than to believe that we could possibly descend to it in a day. The thought of the climb back out again, months later, weak and worn, flashed through my mind and was quickly dismissed.

A sweat-soaked porter passed by under two boxes of oxygen bottles, a 145-pound load and a tough way to make an extra dollar. Norm and I started down through the forests, looking down on the gray and brown tree tops, intricately patterned in their winter nakedness. White islands of blossoming magnolias were beacons in their stark setting and reminded me of dogwood in the Ozark spring. We camped that night on a shelf a short distance below the pass. The moon shone on a haze of rising mist and the smoke of many fires. Beyond the trees, the world spilled into a silvery moonlit cloud on which the ridgetops floated.

Before the night was half begun, the coughing and talking of the porters began, followed too soon by Danu's banging a spoon against a kitchen pan. The crew staggered from the comfort of tents into the damp predawn chill and stood shivering about the sagging metal table. By lantern light we groped for tea, cocoa water, and Metrecal cookies to plaster peanut butter on. With packs and umbrellas we were off, coasting down toward a river hidden in the darkness below. As the sun rose we broke out of the forest, crossed steep tilled fields past thatched farmhouses, and felt the freshness of the new sun give way to the familiar heat of mid-morning until relief came in the humid shade of the jungle. The trail descended in steps made of rocks and tree roots that trapped the dark humus of old leaves; the smell of moist earth was freed by our slipping feet. Ahead in the clearing, smoke rose from the fire. Danu was there with breakfast. The deep rumble of the Dudh Kosi carried easily through the one remaining thicket.

The warmth of the sun, topping off a full breakfast, breeds a certain inertia, at least in those pushing middle age and having a streak of laziness in them, so I lay in the sun shirtless, my face covered. The world was held at a distance; murmuring voices, buzzing flies, the grass tickling the backs of my legs, the momentum of life at a complete standstill. Thoughts floated lazily, as boundless as the clouds, only to be intruded upon by the sound of Jake's voice:

"Can you reach that little nubbin up to the right? It might

take one fingernail." I peered out from under my hat, squinting into the brightness. Barry was glued mysteriously to a wall on the huge boulder at the lower end of the clearing. I watched, wanting to remain uninvolved, as his fingers groped blindly for a handhold, creeping across the smooth granite with sensitive movements of a pianist. At last his hand paused, on something? Then almost magically his body straightened, smoothly and delicately, the edge of his boot biting on a tiny flake and holding. Jake watched quietly, the serious set of his mouth belied by the relaxed grin in his eyes. Then he took to the slab, fingers dancing over the rock, boot edges clinging to imperceptible exfoliations, polishing the rough edges left by Barry's pioneering performance. They were both fine climbers.

Bouldering, when we could find the opportunity, provided a refreshing interlude. It reminded us we were climbers, not merely walkers and that soon we would be called upon to put our climbing to the test. For now, each brief pitch was a puzzle. Following Barry's and Jake's lead, each of us tried to solve it. Dick's arms had never been overstrong for his weight; his power was in his legs. As a result he had developed a fluidness of motion over the years, and his studied control was beautiful to see as he followed after Jake. In contrast, Unsoeld attacked the problem with the same energetic flair with which he faced all challenges, achieving feats of gymnastic contortion with the grunts and groans of a professional wrestler. Before long he was spreadeagled horizontally across the wall, one hand high above, the other pressing downward against smooth rock several inches below his feet. In the end he got there, at the price of an audience completely drained by his skillful brinkmanship. I followed monkey-style, weight too much on my wiry arms and fingers. Will had been studying the rock, jaw muscles contracting as, like a chess player, he plotted each move in advance. Then he attacked with a determination that seemed to say to the rock, "Either I get up or you come down." Our ice climbers, Jim and Lute, gave it a try, mumbling about the beauties of cutting steps up steep ice. Pownall, a superb rock climber, didn't join the game—and even deprived himself of the greater pleasure of being a heckling spectator.

It was slow going the day we moved from Pheriche to Lobuje, climbing the 2,000-foot terminal moraine of the Khumbu Glacier. We were new to the altitude and felt it. At about 16,000 feet, Barry and Jake found a boulder and several people were sitting sluggishly on the hillside looking at it. Altitude itself, I soon discovered, was the challenge in the 15-foot crack Barry had pioneered. Tackling the pitch with naïve enthusiasm, I found myself folding over on the flat summit, prostrate and panting. What a fantastic difference, climbing from 16,000 feet to 16,015! It certainly added a new dimension to bouldering. Porters would come by, set down their loads to watch our antics, then saddle up and shuffle on. One youngster stayed, grinning. We grinned back. "You try?" we asked. Shyly, he came down to the base of the rock, wearing a pair of rotting boots. He attacked

the sharp, narrow crack with a graceless gusto which carried him halfway to the top before he fell off. He laughed, embarrassed, and had at it again, and again. Finally, in frustration, he sat down and removed his boots. As we watched in pained amazement he curled his toes into the knife-edged crack and scampered to the top. He grinned with pride at our cries of "Shabash, well done!" and our predictions about his future as a great high-altitude Sherpa.

We put so many routes up the Lobuje Boulder that there was talk of publishing a guidebook. Coated by a fresh fall of snow, the boulder provided a good training ground for our Sherpas in preparation for the West Ridge. They greeted the practice sessions as children might, jesting, exclaiming, and a little fearful. Uproarious laughter followed when one of them slipped from his holds to dangle at the end of the rope. Many of them climbed with a primitive naturalness that was enviable. It was a universal game.

Yet these scrambles were more than just games for exuberant overripe youth. They were preparation, in a way, for the adulthood that was waiting ahead. Each rock puzzle was a test, though not in a mountaineering sense. Nothing so difficult existed on Everest, on terrain already so well known. This was fortunate, for cold and altitude would make such rock unclimbable. The measure was more of the man than of his climbing ability. Though the performance of others might provide some yardstick, each man faced a solitary challenge. Whether you succeeded or failed on any given pitch, the revelation was in how you faced the challenge, and how Barry did, and Dick and Will. You watched silently, noting the ability of a man to laugh at his own awkwardness. Impatience, self-castigation, the quality rather than the quantity of determination, unreasoning perseverance or reasoning self-appraisal. Impressions were formed, evaluations made and filed away. Competition may have been a part of these games, but if so, it was purely of an individual's own making. There was nothing inherently competitive in climbing from the bottom to the top of a boulder any more than in running the four-minute mile; you were competing only with yourself. In this bouldering seemed to differ from the effort for which it helped prepare. These scrambles were not Everest in miniature; on the mountain competition would almost be forced upon us for two reasons: not everyone would get to the top; all of us wanted to.

Norm broached the question of attitudes toward the summit one evening after dinner. "I'm curious about one thing," he said. "If we're really honest with ourselves, how many of us have real strong hopes, and expect to get to the summit?"

Will Siri scanned the bodies crowded inside the tent. "How many people are there on the team?" he asked in reply.

"Lester, I didn't see your hand up there," said Norm, smiling at our emphatically nonmountaineering psychologist. "But I'm sure that we all know that only a certain number will be able to make it. That's all there is to it logistically; as many as possible, but there are limitations."

"I don't think you've got to worry too much about it," Big Jim replied. "I think the whole team thinks that as long as two men, as long as somebody, gets to the summit, goddammit, that's the important thing."

The only important thing? What about the individual dreams? How do you reconcile the personal ambitions of nineteen climbers with the notion of a group goal which if achieved by some is thereby achieved by all? Nineteen prima donnas could yield a highly explosive mixture. Perhaps appreciation of this fact was enough to prevent detonation. Or was it the realization that no man's hopes could be fulfilled outside the group's goal, that no one could climb Everest alone?

Perhaps a team devoted solely to the expedition objective would be optimal, a group all of whom could say, "It's only important that someone get to the top. I'll do all I can to get him there." Such a philosophy would certainly produce a well-meshed effort. But we were not such a group, and I doubt that such a group would have the same intensity of drive as that attained by a team of personally motivated individuals. With group motivation one extreme, and competitive uncompromising personal desire the other, we fell somewhere between as a team. Two issues helped to clarify where the balance lay: the question of Sherpas on the summit team and the question of West Ridge.

"I think we should also think of what part the Sherpas will play in the final assault," Norm suggested. "I'd like to get some of your reactions and points of view on Sherpas going for the summit. But it should be clear to all that this will diminish each individual's chance to be a member of a summit team."

. . . That anyone should want to climb a high mountain solely for pleasure, is, at the present time, simply not understood by these mountain peasants.

The exceptions are a few Sherpas who have developed a feeling for the beauty of the mountains and have discovered the pleasure of conquering peaks, owing to repeated participation in expeditions. This is especially true in the case of my own Sherpa, Aila, who was my companion for seven years. Often when we were sitting on a summit with a magnificent panorama spread out before us, he would say very dryly, "Very much country, sir." This was his way of expressing his pleasure at the wonderful view. Latterly he went so far as to say, "Very beautiful country, sir." There was a wealth of enthusiasm behind these terse remarks.

—Toni Hagen

"Well, let's ask then," Will said, "if anyone feels Sahibs should have the first crack at the summit if they are able to do so, or whether it should be Sherpa-Sahib teams."

"I think personally Sahibs have the first crack at it, if they are healthy enough to do it," Dave Dingman said.

"At least," said Big Jim, "the Sahib should lead the rope."

"Well, at least be on it," I added.

"Many of these Sherpas have been to the summit of big peaks before; there is no question of their ability," Norman said. "We will strengthen our team if we do figure on Sherpas as members of the climbing team. I think it will strengthen us tremendously."

"If we deny them the opportunity to get to the summit and some of them are able to do so, I think we would make ourselves exceedingly unpopular with the Sherpas," Will said. "Besides, I think we may be overestimating the number of people we're going to put on the summit. Everest is still a high peak and we're not going to be racing everybody up the mountain. I think the chances of getting every one to the summit who would like now to get to the summit are very, very remote. There's one other thing, too. You may not appreciate this yet, but once you start climbing with the Sherpas they'll become far more a part of the team, and friends, than they are on the approach march. There will be less distinction between Sahib and Sherpa."

Jimmy Roberts offered a bit of British logic. "Yes, I think technically now, the Sherpas are quite capable of reaching the summit of Everest, possibly without Sahibs. They like a Sahib along. I'd say there was no necessity to make a political thing of insuring that a Sherpa gets to the summit. I think—just let things take their own course. I think you'll find that one or two Sherpas will reach the summit. I would say that if one Sherpa has got up, and there are two equally fit—a Sahib and a Sherpa, then let the Sahib go. They've had a lot more work to do on the preparation. They deserve it more."

"You know, of course," Norm said, "that the West Ridge will also diminish the number of people who get to the summit. You have to be aware of that."

"I think the probability of that is extremely high," I added. "Presuming that you don't even succeed on the West Ridge, as few as two people could end up climbing the mountain."

"Well, now let's discuss this for a minute," Norm said. "How do you feel about it? Is this fair in a way, to lessen the chances of a certain number of people to get to the top by tackling the West Ridge? Then a lot of guys who are counting heavily on the summit won't have a chance."

Big Jim expressed what most of us thought. "I think that for the good of the Expedition we should have an objective other than just the South Col and the quantity of people on the summit. We should have a new route."

"I would second Jim's point," Will said. This was followed by many nods of agreement. As things stood now, still far from the mountain, there appeared to be a mature balance between personal ambitions and expedition goals.

Whatever weight personal ambition had in this balance, there was one thing that made competition unnecessary. It pertained less to summit hopes than to the myriad challenges of productive day-to-day survival on the mountain. It was the simply lonely question asked in self-appraisal on the boulder. Can I?

5. At Puijan

AT PUIJAN, mist clung to the trees, trapping the damp cold that had sent the rest of the team off to bed. Jake and I sat astride a log, facing each other, and Lute balanced on a stump on the other side of the fire, his sunburnt face glowing redder in the dancing light. Jake had doubts about altitude. Would he be able to hack it high on the West Ridge? Looking at him, I saw myself approaching Masherbrum three years before. I was unsure, a bit afraid then, more confident now, and told him: "I think most people adapt pretty well, as long as they don't get sick. Some come on a little slower than others, like Dick Emerson. But when he finally got going he was plenty strong."

Jake looked skeptical, thinking back to the South Face of McKinley. "I really felt it when we hit the top," he said, "and that's only 20,000."

"But that's a different story. You were moving up a lot faster than we will be here. You couldn't have been very well acclimatized."

"I hope that's the reason." Jake replied.

"Another thing," I continued, "you can't predict who's going to do well from his performance lower down. I suspect there's more than just physiology involved. Take Clinch. There's a guy who wasn't terribly strong, yet he got himself to the summit of Masherbrum. Motivation counts for a hell of a lot. Sometimes the big strong guys who run all over the mountain lower down don't do as well as the scrawny ones up high. If I'm lucky I might even be able to keep up with Jerstad here."

"Drop dead, Hornbein. You don't expect anybody to believe that nonsense, do you?" Lute replied.

"You bet. I could never keep up with you on Rainier."

"How about that day you and Pownall and I battled the blizzard to Cathedral Gap? I was pushing as hard as I could and every time I turned around you were right on my tail."

"Just superb conditioning." I said. "And two liters of oxygen per minute running into the mask I was testing."

"God damn! I didn't know you were using oxygen. No wonder . . ."

"But you'd been high before," Jake said to me. "Isn't that supposed to make it easier next time?"

"That's what they say," I answered, "but it's an old wives' tale. I felt all right on Masherbrum and I'd never been above 14,000 feet before. Only one of the Swiss Everest team had ever been higher than Mont Blanc, and they ran all over the mountain."

"How much difference will oxygen really make?" Lute asked.

"The hardest job," I said, "might just be getting up to the altitude where you start on it. Once you put your mask on you're suddenly down to nineteen or twenty thousand feet inside and that ought to make the rest of the mountain easy."

Lute was dubious about what the extra twenty or thirty pounds load would do; I suspected that we would find oxygen mighty nice on this mountain. To avoid its use was scarcely conceivable, but climbers once felt differently. It would be purer, more meaningful, to climb Everest without such artificial aid. Members of the early British expeditions came within 1,000 feet of the summit, some of them without oxygen; but a long 1,000 feet remained. Their philosophical distaste was reinforced by a vigorous dislike of the heavy and unreliable equipment then available. Now that the equipment problem was solved, we could still easily rationalize ourselves away from purity: Everest was beyond the limits of uphill survival for man without extra oxygen to breathe; the early Everesters themselves had shown that. Speed, safety, and pleasure all decreed the use of oxygen; climbing was supposed to be fun, not suicide.

"At what altitude do we start using it?" Jake asked, thinking back to the evening two weeks before when we had discussed that.

"We're going to spread the oxygen fairly thin," Norm had said. "Didn't we decide we are not going to use oxygen for climbing below the top of the Lhotse Face, Will?"

"Yes."

"Who decided what?" I asked, surprised.

"Below the top of the Lhotse Face?" Bishop asked. "No oxygen until 25,000?"

"Except for sleeping," Norm hastened to add.

The import of the proposal began to sink in slowly.

"That's unrealistic on the West Ridge," said Bishop.

"I think it's unrealistic on both routes," I said, "if you want to . . ."

"There goes you physiology project, Will," Norman interrupted.

". . . to me it's a mistake not to use oxygen when we start up the Lhotse Face," I finished.

"I'm going to argue against that," Will replied.

"I know you can climb higher," I said. "We've done it. Lots of people have climbed a lot higher, but to prolong performance at high altitude, especially if we are climbing two routes and need every man we can get, I think it's a mistake not to use oxygen at the same levels that it's been used by the Swiss and British in the past."

"Will, what will that do to your project?" Norm asked.

"Well, if you start at 22,000 feet you're going to wreck it."

"Well, I wasn't figuring 22,000," I replied. "I was figuring to start from Camp 3, the camp that's just a little above the bottom of the Lhotse Face."

Norman did a bit of quick recollection. "Camp 3 is 22,800 feet."

"Yes, 23,000," I said, rounding off.

It was Will Siri's turn, "We can not use oxygen below 23,000 feet or we're going to muck up the whole business. The summit of Everest, I agree, is an important objective; but don't forget that the expedition got under way because of scientific objectives as well. Without carrying out the scientific objectives we can't come back with something we can justify this trip with."

Suddenly Dan Doody came to life, expressing the concern of many in the group. "Yes, but now we're getting back to science versus climbing. Our scientific projects were supposedly designed so that they wouldn't interfere with the climbing at all."

"It's not," Will said. "Except on this one point. If we start using oxygen . . ."

"This is an important point," Dan interrupted. "I think it ought to be discussed."

"If you say we can't use it below 23,000 feet that presents no problem," I said. "We'll just try a little harder to make sure that camp gets closer to 23,000 and then we'll start using it there."

Unsoeld smiled and said, "We could let Will go out two hundred feet above camp and put up a red flag. That's where we switch on."

"You can do without oxygen at this altitude if you're well acclimatized," Norm said.

"The point is," I answered, "that when you're first going to work up there, you're not so well acclimatized, and you get a great deal of benefit out of it. It undoubtedly increases your staying power and reduces deterioration."

"But Will's point is a very important one," Norm continued. "There's always a danger that once we're on the mountain, we'll get all excited and forget about science. We can't because that's where a lot of our backing came from. We'd be definitely dishonest, we'd be crooks, downright crooks, if we just threw it out the window. We can't."

"We can't throw the summit out the window either," Dan said, and Norm came back, "Now wait a second Dan, let's . . ." and I interrupted:

"I don't think that this represents much of a difference of opinion, and I don't think anybody is going to get carried away using oxygen below that altitude because we don't have the oxygen for it anyway."

Smiling, I asked Will, "Would it be better not to use it at all?"

"Well, frankly, yes. I hope you all realize that the more you knock yourselves out the better it will be for the study."

Barry Prather was taken by the thought. "Nobody's climbed this mountain without oxygen yet, have they?"

"Without what?" Norm asked.

"Everybody that's climbed the mountain has used oxygen haven't they?" Barry repeated.

"What are you thinking of, Bear?" Willi asked.

"Why not?"

"Just wait, you'll find out," was my reply.

Will Siri said, "It has already been established as Expedition policy, I believe, isn't that right Norman, that no one will climb above the South Col without oxygen?"

"Beyond the shadow of a doubt," Norm answered. "Nobody will climb without oxygen."

"And if you do climb to the summit without oxygen, don't came back," Dan put in.

"Or let Lester get a base line I.Q. study on you anyway," I added, considering the possibility of brain damage at such altitudes.

"I feel there is really a lot of playing it by ear in the wind," Maynard Miller said.

"I don't want to play with my ear," Gil Roberts replied.

"Especially not in a high wind," said Barry.

"I think it's clear that if we climb the mountain, we'll do it with oxygen," Norm said, "but if we use oxygen too low we're going to defeat this project. If we wait too high we're going to defeat—ourselves."

"We can try to keep its use to a minimum," I said, "and this is logistically worthwhile, but with the understanding that when it seems indicated at 23,000 feet we'll be able to use it."

Will agreed.

The discussion had ended about there. Now, apparently, Jake thought the fire needed oxygen. He poked at it vigorously, sending showers of sparks floating skyward with the smoke. Each tiny light danced among the branches of the trees, to disappear in the mist. There were still many questions and many doubts; assurances would not put them to rest. The answer would come only on the mountain; for Jake, for Lute, for me, for all of us.

Narrative continues on page 101

The light died in the low clouds. Falling snow drank in the dusk. Shrouded in silence, the branches wrapped me in their peace. When the boundaries were erased, once again the wonder: that *I* exist.

—DAG HAMMARSKJOLD

The Sherpas of the Khumbu Region

... The Sherpas of eastern Nepal have a sense of a distinct ethnic identity which clearly sets them apart from other high altitude dwellers of Tibetan stock. ...

The principal concentration of the Sherpas is in the three regions of Khumbu, Pharak and Solu. Khumbu, which stretches from the Tibetan border to the confluence of the Dudh Kosi and the Bhote Kosi is a region where the villages lie at an average altitude of 12,000 to 13,000 feet, and summer settlements and grazing grounds extend above the 16,000-foot line. Pharak is the narrow strip of country lying to both sides of the Dudh Kosi between its confluence with the Bhote Kosi and the gorge above Jubing. In this area the villages lie on the banks of the river, as well as on broad, gently-sloping ledges high above the level of the Dudh Kosi. Solu, which is the Nepali name for an area known in Sherpa as Shar-rang, lies south-west of Pharak, and includes the broad valley of the Solu River and several side valleys. Here there are no deep gorges as there are in Khumbu and Pharak, and the gentle slopes offer better prospects for large-scale cultivation. The collective term Solu-Khumbu or Shar-Khumbu is sometimes used for the entire area consisting of the three regions of Khumbu, Pharak and Solu. ...

Although the population of Khumbu represents only a fraction of the total number of Sherpas, it is a group of vital importance for an understanding of the characteristic features of the Sherpa way of life. For in the high valleys of Khumbu, remote from the influence of the peoples inhabiting the middle ranges of Nepal, Sherpa society and culture has developed on its own lines: adaptation to an inclement habitat has led to intensive specialization in such economic activities as yak-breeding and trade with Tibet; the great distances that separate Khumbu from the centres of state administration have allowed the growth of a particular type of local government and authority system; and close contact with Buddhist monasteries beyond the Himalayan main range has favoured the development of religious institutions, so that today Khumbu can boast of monasteries that enjoy a reputation even beyond the frontiers of Nepal.

The pattern of Sherpa settlement in the Khumbu region has been shaped by a climate and an environment which precludes the possibility of combining mixed farming with a sedentary way of life. No single locality above the confluence of the Dudh Kosi and the Bhote Kosi possesses resources which alone would enable its inhabitants to maintain themselves and their livestock throughout the year. In order to secure a constant supply of food for his animals the yak-owner must continually move with his herds from pasture to pasture; and the Sherpa owning no cattle must supplement his income from the tillage of the soil by extensive trading excursions. Neither can afford to spend the greater part of the year in one place. ...

The availability of arable land is not the only factor determining a site's suitability as a main village. There must be a perennial source of water and an adequate supply of firewood within reasonable reach. Settlements such as Dingpoche in the upper Imja Khola Valley, which lie at too great a distance from the nearest wood-reserves, are not suitable as sites for main villages, even though there may be sufficient arable land and ample water. ...

Religious buildings are found in all main villages. Temples or structures housing prayer-wheels, either alone or in groups, occupy a central position. ... Other religious edifices found in all main villages, as well as occasionally in subsidiary settlements and on passes far removed from human habitation, are stupa-like *chorten* and *mani*—isolated natural rocks or slabs of stone assembled in wall-like formations, each of which bears an inscription in Tibetan characters. ... A Sherpa village consists not only of homesteads and individually owned, walled-in gardens, fields and meadows, but also of pasture and forest-land held jointly by the community. All villages are entitled to utilize the village lands, but the exploitation of the produce growing on them is carefully controlled. At altitudes above 12,000 feet wood is a scarce commodity and trees growing within village boundaries may only be felled for specific purposes; firewood must be brought from more distant areas. Pastures in the vicinity of villages are liable to over-grazing, and whereas every villager has the right to graze his cattle and cut grass for storage as winter fodder on common land, the village assembly, meeting at least once a year, decides which areas must be kept clear of cattle during the ensuing months so as to allow for a period of recuperation. ...

Subsidiary settlements of another category are those known as *yersa* or *phu*. Their role is altogether different. Situated in the vicinity of high pastures, many of them above the tree-line, they comprise dwelling houses and walled-in meadows; in all except the very highest there are also a few potato plots which are planted and harvested later than those in the main village. The grass growing on the walled-in meadows is cut and dried; and the hay stored for use as fodder in the autumn and spring when the surrounding terrain is covered in snow. ... The highest *yersa* in the Mount Everest region are Lobuche (16,175 ft.) close to the Khumbu Glacier and Chukhung (15,978 ft.) on the Imja Khola. Another such settlement at great altitude is Gokyo (about 15,600 ft.), which lies on the shores of the Gokyo glacial lake, close to the source of the Dudh Kosi. ... Similar in purpose to the *yersa*, but different in form are encampments known as *resa*. These consist of roughly built stone walls, which when occupied are temporarily roofed with yak-hair blankets or bamboo mats. Serving the herdsmen as shelter on pastures where it is convenient to graze cattle for a few days, but where there is no site suitable for a more permanent settlement, they are found at very great altitudes, sometimes above the highest *yersa*, and again at fairly low levels, sometimes so close to the main village that they are within easy walking distance. While children can be entrusted with the task of herding during the daytime, adults need only spend the night in the *resa* and so be at hand to guard the cattle against attack by wolves or leopards.

Ownership of property in *gunsa* and *yersa* settlements is an indispensable concomitant of yak-breeding. Without such dispersed holdings it is not possible to maintain even a moderately-sized herd, and all yak-owners spend a large part of the year moving with their herds from one subsidiary settlement to another. . . . Families, whose main livelihood is gained in agricultural pursuits, find it equally advantageous to extend their agricultural activities over plots situated at varying altitudes, where crops are planted and harvested earlier and later than in the main villages. . . .

During six months of the year the soil of Khumbu is frozen and all agricultural operations are at a standstill. While the Sherpas of Pharak and Solu cultivate winter wheat and barley, and sow in early summer buckwheat, maize and potatoes, the inhabitants of Khumbu must be content with the produce of one agricultural season. The choice of crops that can be cultivated at an altitude of 13,000-14,000 ft. is limited. In most of Khumbu only buckwheat, potatoes, white turnips and a spinach-like vegetable are grown, but in the high valley of Dingpoche where there are possibilities of irrigation, the Sherpas have succeeded in raising a type of bearded, short-stemmed barley. . . .

During the summer months agricultural work in the main villages comes to a standstill, for at this time of the year most Khumbu Sherpas are living in subsidiary settlements. Family members are scattered over a wide area: the men remain with the herds on the high pastures until the middle of September but women are engaged in lifting potatoes from mid-August, first in low-lying *gunsa* settlements and then in the main villages. . . . The cutting of buckwheat starts as soon as the potatoes are out of the ground. Men and women cut the crop with sickles and beat out the grain on threshing floors situated in the fields. The harvesting of potatoes in *yersa* settlements is done after the harvests in the main villages have been gathered; it is at this time that those Sherpas who own land in Dingpoche go there to reap the barley. This is not cut, but pulled out by the roots and spread out on the ground to dry. . . .

While agriculture provides the Sherpas with the bulk of their food supply, the breeding of yak and other cattle allows them to supplement their diet with milk products, and to engage in the profitable cattle trade that is transacted between Solu and Tibet. Khumbu, because of its geographical position and its climate and the availability of extensive high altitude grazing grounds, holds a key position in this flourishing business. . . .

The efforts of all cattle-owners are directed towards the production of butter. Great quantities are needed for domestic as well as for ritual use. Butter is eaten with, or as part of, the more highly valued foods; it is used as fuel in the butter lamps lit at all Buddhist ceremonies, and is moulded into various shapes for the decoration of sacrificial dough figures. Butter is also used as a medium for the payment of wages, and it forms an important article of trade in the Tibetan market. . . .

The second important product of yak is hair. Yak are shorn once a year, usually in June or July. . . . Though Sherpas are not supposed to kill animals they are not averse to eating the meat of animals which die by accident or are slaughtered by others. Professional butchers of *hyawo* class come once a year from Tibet for this purpose. . . . Yak's blood provides the Sherpas with another type of food. The blood, drawn from the jugular vein of the living animal, is mixed with salt and left to coagulate. It may be eaten raw with *tsampa,* or cut into strips and fried.

Besides contributing milk, meat and blood for the Sherpas' diet, and providing hair for blankets and textiles, yak serve as the principle means of transporting goods. In the trade with Tibet they are used as pack-animals and in the seasonal migrations they carry a householder's belongings from settlement to settlement. *Yak, nak* and *zopkio* are all accustomed to carrying loads and the normal weight is between 100 and 120 lb. distributed in two packs. The animals are easy to handle and two men are sufficient to take a train of ten or twelve across the Nangpa La. . . .

In Khumbu there is only a limited occupational specialization according to crafts. The Sherpas do not share the Nepalese Hindus' attitude to certain types of manual work. Except for such activities as slaughtering animals, which is sinful for the strict Buddhist, there is no occupation a Sherpa would consider polluting or demeaning. . . . Thus the bootmaker or expert carpenter provides services which are beyond the ability of the ordinary householder, and in this respect his role is not different from that of the carver in stone employed to carve the sacred formula, *Om mani padme hum,* into a rock-face or of the painter commissioned to paint frescoes in temples or private chapels. . . .

In recent years a novel type of specialization in the shape of work for mountaineering expeditions has offered to poor and energetic young men new chances of economic gain. Normally a Sherpa without land or capital cannot hope to attain more than a modest prosperity even by a lifetime of hard work. The structure of Sherpa economics favours the entrepreneur rather than the wage-earner, and for the impecunious many years of working in the pay of others must precede the acquisition of land and cattle, or the first steps as an independent trader. But the successful high-altitude porter may return after a single season's climbing with sufficient cash to set up his own business or to buy his first plot of land.

The sudden affluence of those who engage in expedition work has brought to the fore a class of men who were used to living in the shadow of families whose status was backed by inherited wealth. This has created a situation which may well result in far-reaching social and economic changes. On the whole it can be said that the porter element has not yet displaced the members of the traditional status groups who provide the leadership of the villages, for the rest of the community tends to view with some suspicion a sudden rise to prominence which is dependent on spheres outside the framework of their traditional culture. Moreover long years of work for expeditions tend to develop egocentric attitudes in the individual which accord ill with Sherpa ideals of behaviour. That the earnings from work on mountaineering expeditions has been beneficial to many families of Khumbu cannot be doubted, but the prolonged absence of young men from Khumbu has resulted in a vacuum which can only be filled by immigrant labour from Tibet.

All Sherpas share the tradition of having immigrated from Tibet but the circumstances and time of this migration are obscure. While the subsequent arrival and miraculous feats of various lamas are the subject of numerous legends, traditions

NORMAN G. DYHRENFURTH: *High yak pasture, Bhota Kosi Valley*

and myths relating to the Sherpas' migration to the regions of Khumbu and Solu and of the establishment of the present villages are almost completely lacking. . . . There is, however, fairly general agreement that the ancestors of all Sherpa clans (*rhu*) arrived in the area at approximately the same time and that ever since the number of clans has remained constant. . . .

The essential feature of the Sherpa clan is its role as the basic exogamous unit. All Sherpas of the same *rhu*, irrespective of the distance which may separate their villages and the impossibility of tracing consanguinity, consider themselves as agnatic kin and debarred from marriage. . . .

In every Sherpa village of Khumbu men known as *naua* are appointed to control the use of village lands for purposes of agriculture, silviculture and cattle-breeding. Their function is to hold a balance between the needs of these branches of Sherpa economy, to husband the communal resources and to prevent damage to the interests of the community by the careless or egotistic behaviour of individuals. . . .

Besides the *naua* responsible for the control of the movements of the cattle and their co-ordination with the work on the fields there are in every village officials in charge of the preservation of the tree growth on the common lands of the village. These officials are also known as *naua,* but as they deal with the husbanding of the community's wood and timber resources, they are referred to as *shingo-naua, shing* being the Sherpa word for wood.

The *shingo-naua* are appointed every year; though the term of their office is usually twelve months, *shingo-naua* who have proved efficient and are popular may be confirmed in office over a number of years. Two to four *shingo-naua* are appointed for each village, the number being dictated by local conditions, i.e. by the size of the village and the extent of lands to be protected; the number must, however, by sufficient to allow them to exercise a continual vigilance and thus to prevent woodcutters from encroaching on the protected areas. It is within the competence of the *shingo-naua* to permit limited fellings for specific purposes such as house-building, and they do not interfere with the cutting of wood required for funeral pyres. Firewood must be brought from more distant areas and during their term of office the *naua* are entitled to check woodstacks if they suspect that these contain wood taken from prohibited areas.

The fining of offenders takes place annually soon after the O-sho rite when the *shingo-naua* call the villagers to a meeting at the public assembly place. At this meeting all those guilty of forest offences during the previous year must bring a bottle of beer and admit their guilt publicly. If the offence is of a minor nature, such as the cutting of a few green branches in an area where only dead wood may be collected, the beer is accepted as adequate recompense, but cash fines are imposed for more serious breaches of the law. . . .

. . . The following list of sins [was] enumerated spontaneously by one of my lay informants: to quarrel, steal, cheat in trade; talk ill of another behind his back, particularly if that which is related is not true; to kill any living creature (and even a butcher whose profession it is to slaughter yak and sheep sins in so doing, but those who buy the meat do not); to have sexual relations with the spouse of another, or with a nun or a monk because the party involved contributes to the sin committed by a celibate; to threaten children or make them cry whatever the reason; to marry a girl who is unwilling is a sin both for the husband and for the parents who arranged the marriage; to hit an animal, to fell trees, though on occasion it is inevitable, to pluck flowers or to set fire to the forest; for monks and nuns it is sin to drink too much and become intoxicated; and to cause a spirit long associated with a locality to be driven out is sin for the person who commissions the exorcising, but not for the lama who executes it.

The Sherpas' approach to moral problems reflects their great respect for the dignity and independence of the individual. Any action encroaching forcibly on this independence is considered sin. Respect for the independence of the individual is expressed also in the attitude to those known to have committed sins. Their actions are held to be their own affair, and no public notice is taken of what is recognized as a violation of the moral code.

Sherpa ideology equates knowledge and virtue. A lama's reputation of saintliness is proportionate to his learning, for the Sherpa believes that an intellectual grasp of the true doctrine must necessarily lead to correct conduct. They emphasize, however, that purity of heart is more important than a knowledge of the scriptures and the performance of elaborate and costly rites.

Although the expenditure of material wealth for religious ends can never replace purity of heart, the liberal giving away of earthly goods gives rise to admiration. Not the accumulation, but the proper utilization of wealth, lends a person prestige, and there is a certain analogy between the meritorious use of material resources, and the ideal way of utilizing accumulated *sönam,* or religious merit. Just as Sherpas expect that a rich man will on certain occasions, such as memorial feasts for close relatives, distribute a large part of his wealth to the lamas engaged in the performance of the rites and to his co-villagers attending the celebrations, so they assume that a saintly lama, whose accumulation of *sönam* would enable him to enter Devachen, the realm of eternal bliss, will voluntarily forgo this enviable fate and accept a new incarnation in order to devote his wisdom and his saintliness to the service of humanity. The liberal expenditure of material as well as spiritual resources for the benefit of one's fellow-men represents an ideal which explains many facets of the Sherpa's social conduct. Compassion with all animate creatures is in their eyes the essence of every virtue, and selfless activity in the wider interest of humanity complements the striving for personal spiritual perfection.

—Christoph von Fürer-Haimendorf

in *Mount Everest: Formation, Population and Exploration of the Everest Region* (Oxford, 1963)

RICHARD M. EMERSON: Yak above Imja Khola Valley; Tamserku in background

. . . On each day's march we were to find the day made memorable either by some little incident, almost always trivial, or by a sight so briefly seen that we could not have imagined that any indelible record would be left on the memory. But so it was. We moved daily through scenes of the most spendid beauty; daily, on every hand and wherever we might turn, there it was manifested, so that we became familiar with beauty and took its presence very much for granted, and ceased consciously to respond: until that daily, fleeting glimpse into the heart of beauty's very self came suddenly upon the inner eye—flashed upon the soul—and was gone. The duration of vision is of no consequence. . . .

RICHARD M. EMERSON: Stream crossing in rain, above Dudh Kosi Valley

I tried to let their beauty soak in, and when I did so a new beauty, something additional to all I had yet seen, seemed to shine out of them; out of the grass an added richness of green, out of the pines more fragrance of resin, from the blossom of the rhododendrons a glow of colour still brighter; unfathomable deeps and gentleness bloomed in the sky's blue. . . .

This newness taken on by the world was like that of something freshly created. Its loveliness had youth and vigour and an immortality so obviously not of its manifested self, but of that ever new and ancient beauty, wherein all individual things have being and life, and which they serve. Five thousand feet under me, from the dark greens of the Nandakini Gorge up to the brown tip of the lammergeyer's wing, turned to the sky where it wheeled in thin pure air, and in all that lay between, there was displayed the overwhelming harmony of things sharply strange and separate, that fully and from their beginning were entered into one another and oned. How clearly this integrating principle of the universe disposed and flung forth His power that morning. His name men called God, or the Infinite One, Beauty or Truth, according to the context in which His works happen to be seen.

—W. H. MURRAY

RICHARD M. EMERSON: *Cloud forest detail*

One generation passeth away, and another generation cometh: but
the earth abideth for ever.

The sun also ariseth, and the sun goeth down, and hasteth to
his place where he arose.

The wind goeth toward the south, and turneth about unto the north;
it whirleth about continually, and the wind returneth again according
to his circuits.

All the rivers run into the sea; yet the sea is not full; unto
the place from whence the rivers come, thither they return again.

—Ecclesiastes

. . . Beyond and below, the Sarju flashed under the next great rise of the hills. I had the sense of emerging from a long, dark tunnel. The hectic, bewildering weeks of preparation, the stupefying meals of the voyage out, the hustle at Bombay and bustle at Ranikhet—they were all like the wild waters of a subterranean stream, in the navigation of which we had been too busy to think. And how the stream burst from its tunnel on to the open slopes of the Himalaya. It cast us out into sunshine. For a moment dazzled, we suddenly saw spread before us a world made new. All the senses of the soul were not so much refreshed as reborn, as though after death. We were free men once again, for the first time in months really able to live in the present moment.

—W. H. MURRAY

GIL ROBERTS: Gorge near Namche Bazar

. . . the mountains speak in wholly different accents to those who have paid in the service of toil for the right of entry to their inner shrines.

It is the mind which compels the rock climber to despise the gross security of the plain and it is the sense of dominion of the mind over the body which explains the almost godlike happiness of the climber as he coaxes from some smooth forbidding cliff the harmony of scanty foot and handhold which enable him to defy the downward drag of the sheer emptiness below his feet.

. . . we should make every effort to win recruits for sports which bring man into the closest touch with unspoiled nature. The mountains and the sea are great avenues of adventure precisely because the mountaineer and the seaman have to study something of greater value than the habits of the internal combustion engine.

—Sir Arnold Lunn

In a hundred ages of the gods, I could not tell thee of the glories of Himachal. As the dew is dried up by the morning sun, so are the sins of mankind by the sight of Himachal.

—*The Skanda Purana*

Remember thy Creator in the days of thy youth. Rise free from care before the dawn, and seek adventures. Let the noon find thee by other lakes, and the night overtake thee everywhere at home. There are no larger fields than these, no worthier games than may here be played.

—HENRY DAVID THOREAU

. . . For how great the pleasure, how great, think you, are the joys of the spirit, touched as is fit it should be, in wondering at the mighty mass of mountains while gazing upon their immensity and, as it were, in lifting one's head among the clouds. In some way or other the mind is overturned by their dizzying height and is caught up in contemplation of the Supreme Architect. Those, to be sure, whose spirits are sluggish wonder at nothing; they remain idly at home, do not enter the theatre of the universe, hide in a corner like dormice in the winter, do not consider that the human race has been established in the world in order that from its marvels it might infer a something greater, namely the Supreme Divine Will itself. With such sloth do they toil that like swine they are forever staring at the earth, never gazing with uplifted face at the heavens, nerve holding aloft their countenances to the stars. Let such, therefore, wallow in the mire, let them lie stupefied amid gains and sordid pursuits. The followers of wisdom will proceed to contemplate with the eyes of the body and the spirit the sights of this earthly paradise: among which are by no means of least account the steep and lofty slopes of mountains, their inaccessible precipices, the hugeness of their flanks stretching to heaven, their high crags, their dark forests.

—CONRAD GESNER (1541)

. . . the boy, Gesner, came into a world of amazing change. Little more than sixty years had passed since the fall of Constantinople ended the line of Roman emperors, and scarcely a generation since Columbus reached strange shores—the end of the Middle Ages. In printing, the incunabula period had just closed. Leonardo da Vinci, father of experimental science, was still living, an old man in a new world, while Copernicus was not yet ready to publish his dangerously novel theory of the earth and planets wheeling around the sun. The voices which stirred the land were those of Luther and Calvin. Yet the Renaissance was not a sudden break with the mysticism and authority of the Middle Ages, but rather a gradual, inevitable result of a series of circumstances favorable to the development of new ideas.

—J. MONROE THORINGTON

I say therefore that he is an enemy of nature, whosoever has not deemed lofty mountains to be most worthy of great contemplation. Surely the height of the more elevated mountains seems already to have risen above a baser lot and to have escaped from our storms, as though lying within another world. There the force of the most powerful sun, of the air and of the winds is not the same. The snows linger perpetually, the softest of objects, which melts even at the touch of the fingers, recks not at all for any glow or violence of the sun's heat: nor vanishes with time but rather freezes into the most enduring ice and everlasting crystal. . . .

. . . Whatever in other places nature offers here and there but sparingly, in the mountains she presents everywhere and in sufficiency as though in a heap so to speak, she spreads it out, unfolds it, and sets before the eye all her treasure, all her jewels. And so of all the elements and the variety of nature the supreme wonder resides in the mountains. In these it is possible to see "the burden of the mighty earth," just as if nature were vaunting herself & making trial of her strength . . .

—CONRAD GESNER (1541)

How great the pleasure, how great think you are the joys of the spirit touched in wondering at the mighty mass of mountains when gazing at their immensity and, as it were, in lifting one's head among the clouds. In some way or other the mind is caught up in contemplation of the Supreme Architect.

—CONRAD GESNER, 1543

AL AUTEN: Looking down on Thyangboche, Kwangde in distance
THOMAS HORNBEIN: Thyangboche lamasery and Everest

The peasants and the tourists are equally transient where the mountains wrestle and sleep. They will certainly outlive the Atomic Age and will perhaps outlast the life of man himself. "The mountains from their heights reveal two truths," so wrote Hilaire Belloc, "They suddenly make us feel our insignificance and at the same time they free the immortal mind, and let it feel its greatness, and they release it from the earth."

—VIVIAN H. GREEN

The moon shone with the greatest splendour in the midst of an ebon-black sky. . . . What a moment for contemplation! For how much pain and privation do such moments not compensate! The soul rises up, the horizons of the spirit seem to widen, and from the midst of this majestic silence one seems to hear the voice of Nature and to become the confidant of her most secret actions.

—DR. PACCARD (1786)
quoted by Gaston Rebuffat

There I lay staring upward, while the stars wheeled over. . . . Faint to my ears came the gathered rumour of all lands: the springing and the dying, the song and the weeping, and the slow everlasting groan of overburdened stone.

—J. R. R. TOLKIEN

RICHARD M. EMERSON: *Thyangboche in snow*

. . . Until one is committed there is hesitancy, the chance to draw back, always ineffectiveness. Concerning all acts of initiative (and creation), there is one elementary truth, the ignorance of which kills countless ideas and splendid plans: that the moment one definitely commits oneself, then Providence moves too. All sorts of things occur to help one that would never otherwise have occurred. A whole stream of events issues from the decision, raising in one's favour all manner of unforeseen incidents and meetings and material assistance, which no man could have dreamt would have come his way. I have learned a deep respect for one of Goethe's couplets:

> Whatever you can do, or dream you can, begin it.
> Boldness has genius, power, and magic in it.

—W. H. MURRAY

6. Thyangboche

THE monotonous chanting floated from the gompa, softened by distance and the new fallen snow. Occasionally, horns would add impetus to the prayers racing heavenward. Shafts of evening sunlight behind the monastery gave it a new splendor. The place seemed in perfect harmony with the wild mountain walls that embraced it. A thousand feet below, the Imja Khola snaked about the base of the ridge, carrying the melt from the summit of the world. Ice-sheathed walls soared high, a pattern of delicate flutings and translucent knife-edged arêtes. Here man seemed to be reaching for something. His grip was tenuous, inconsequential, yet full of beauty and meaning. His was a world of peace wrought from wildness and latent power. The wildness culminated above the prayer flags, above the immense granite walls of Nuptse—up there on the highest point on earth. Framed by dissolving cloud, it hung suspended in space, the final pyramid burning golden in the evening light. The summit plume raced eastward, yet could not free itself from the solid bastion which gave it birth.

The lamas of Thyangboche lived in enviable purpose. They were not halfway to heaven; they were *there*, their lives spent searching, probing the why of existence, seeking understanding. And maybe understanding could be found here, even of the thing that prevented my staying to seek it.

That night Willi and I walked in the new-fallen snow. We were surrounded by peaks glittering silver in the moonlight: Thamserku and Kangtega, rising almost straight above our heads, the jewel of Ama Dablam shining, and the dark rock of Everest half-sensed over the Nuptse wall. It was a crisp, still night, as we stomped through the knee-deep snow. Chanting came from the monastery, and the rhythmical thump-shuffle of dancing Sherpa feet from a nearby house, turning our awareness to the world of men enclosed within.

"By daylight, the scene is no less wonderful," I wrote. "Frustratingly so, for I am at a loss to know how to capture it. The summit is there, and seems a long way off, now out of cloud. My mood is one of midafternoon lethargy, troubled by a macroscopic awe of my microscopic role in the scheme of things above me.

"Desire for our goal seems terribly strong, or else the dreams I've always cherished are coming more and more vividly close to reality. Emerson caught me gazing carefully and plottingly at a photo in Hunt's book of the route from Advance Base to the West Shoulder, and chided me for perusing something to which we had both already devoted all the time and discussion imaginable. I smiled sheepishly and turned to a *Playboy* which showed up in our Base Camp food supply."

I was not alone. Dave's question had been planted and answers had grown: personal desire had separated us into what would ultimately be two expeditions if an attempt on the West Ridge proved feasible.

With clear weather, the snow vanished almost as fast as it had come. In the sunlit warmth we looked long through Bishop's telephoto lens at the upper fifteen hundred feet of Everest, analyzing each detail of its left-hand skyline, plotting camps, speculating on the route and the problems the down-sloping limestone posed on that side of the mountain. Filing by the soggy remains of a once well-stacked snow woman Jim Whittaker had created, to the delight of the Sherpas. We sought a corner of sunny isolation for a planning session. There were seven West Ridgers now: Dick, Jake, Dave, Barry Corbet, Barry Bishop (Barrel), Willi, and I.

The expedition had long before decided that once Advance Base was established, a reconnaissance to determine feasibility of the West Ridge should be the first order of business. We West Ridgers convinced ourselves that it would be best to send up the four "old Himalayan hands," Willi, Dick, Barrel, and me to do the sleuthing—logic underlain by our own personal desire.

Willi wondered, "Should we send up a bunch of old broken-down crocks on as vigorous a push as this? You could burn yourself out on this reconnaissance. All I can say is that we had better depend on not burning out."

Dick agreed, and said, "The recon is going to be very early in the game."

"Yes," Willi said. "You won't be acclimatized to the Cwm even, and you're going to be busting trail up to 22,000 or 23,000. That can really wear you down. I'd welcome any comments on the makeup of the team, whether you think this is a likely combination or if we ought to include Barry or Jake or Dave, and drop one of us."

"The composition of the team is sound, I think," Dave said, "on the basis of experience."

"O.K. Let me ask one question," Dick said. "In the event that I'm not on the team, I would like to send my little Minifon recorder with someone to record your deliberation."

"You've just insured your participation in this affair—no matter how sick you might be," I answered.

Jake broke his usual silence: "Would it be feasible to have more than four on the initial reconnaissance?"

"The idea is to decide whether the route is worth messing with," I answered. "To do this, ideally we should surmount the step at 25,000—or at least be pretty damned sure it's passable. You need no more than four men, possibly as few as two. The number of possibilities along that step and the magnitude of the decision for the whole expedition suggest it is most desirable to have two ropes of two and possibly exchange routes on consecutive days to get a really well-founded opinion."

"What we decide on the recon," Willi said, "will probably be the most important decision made on the entire expedition as far as we can foresee. Once we split into two routes we will have endangered the summit. The whole expedition could go down the drain."

"But it will have been fun," Jake volunteered.

"How far above the shoulder do you think you can go in a day?" asked Dave.

RICHARD M. EMERSON: Detail, melting snow
THOMAS HORNBEIN: Waterfall, Imja Khola, between Thyangboche and Pangboche

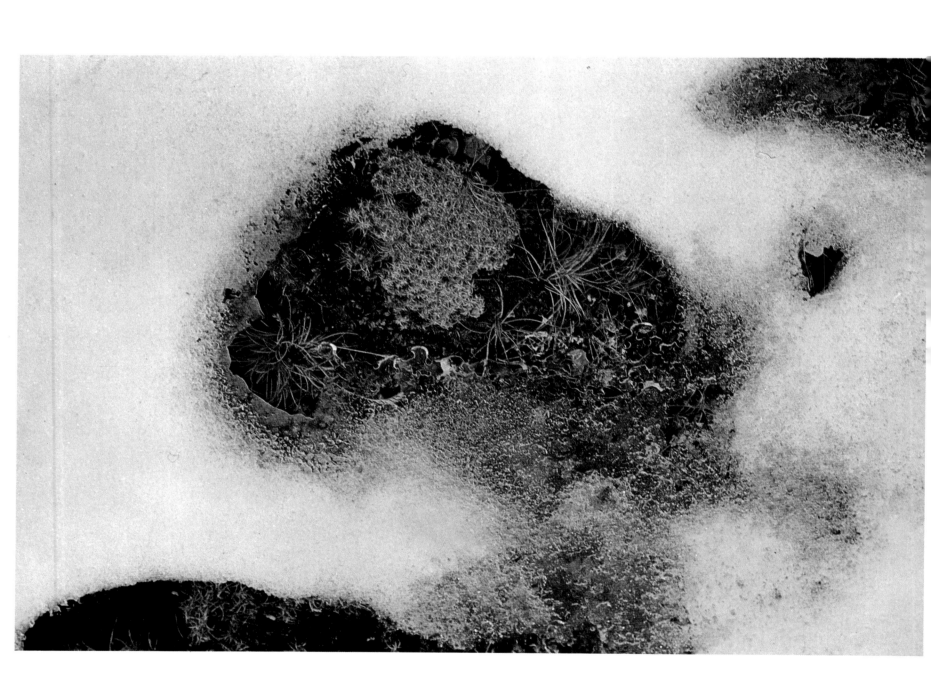

"At that stage of acclimatization it will be a miracle if we can do fifteen hundred feet," Willi replied.

Untroubled by reality, I dissented. "If we go up that snow gully over there we can do three thousand in a day."

"You'd better have somebody along," Dick said, "to temper Unsoeld's enthusiasm for that crazy avalanche trap of a couloir."

"I hope you mean Hornbein," Willi corrected, trying to shuck himself of any connection with such a far-left route (it was a mile out into Communist China).

"That's right—Hornbein's couloir," Dick corrected himself. "I'm sorry."

Our idea of the route was based upon photos a few of us had studied weeks before back in the States, but we had no pictures with us now, only our imaginations. Unfortunately, Unsoeld's picture was different from mine.

"Unsoeld is a deviate to the right, I'm afraid," I said with an air of superiority.

"I'm sort of a middle-of-the-road advocate myself," Dick said.

"There goes straight-up-the-rock-wall Emerson," I replied.

Barry attempted a severe frown. "I don't know about sending all these wild men up there."

"There's this urge, as you approach the twilight years," Willi replied, "to go out in a blaze of glory." Returning to the original issue, he said. "You really have to press hard out there to cross the slabs of the North Face. You'd presumably have to try to get as far as the avalanche trap."

"Just a minute. Let's change the terminology," I said, objecting to his description of the couloir.

"Very well; as far as Hornbein's avalanche trap. You'd have to snoop pretty strongly up that. You might have to take two days. There's also the other side of the whole damned Ridge."

"Hornbein's route is in another country, if anybody cares anything about that," Barry reminded us.

"That shouldn't be a mountaineering consideration," I said. "Mountaineering should know no boundary lines."

"Wouldn't it be interesting," Willi wondered, "if the Chinese were on the mountain this year, too? I don't suppose anybody would have heard about it."

Jake asked, "Our job would be to put in Camp 5 and 6? Is this correct?"

"Your job would be to establish Camp 4 and find a route to Camp 5," Willi answered. "The general theory for operating on the Ridge would be in two-man teams plus Sherpas. We'd have three teams working in leapfrog fashion."

"If everybody is in good health, we could have four teams," Dave suggested.

"There's going to have to be a continuous rebalancing between routes," I said. "The thing that could hurt us is if things get really rough on the Col route we may lose personnel. We could stand the loss less well than they could."

"Yes," said Barry. "On the other route I'm almost convinced that if all the Sahibs get sick, the route can still go ahead about the same."

"Or faster," someone said.

Jake sat scratching profiles of the mountain in the dirt with a stick. Barrel, remembering that this was meant to be a planning

session asked, "Have logistics been worked out about hardware, ladders, fixed ropes?"

"Yes," I replied. "We've started, for the recon group."

"Do you know how many wire ladders we've got?" Barrel asked.

"Ninety feet," was Barry's answer. "Six fifteen-footers."

Dick looked a bit alarmed. "That isn't too much."

"Maynard mentioned he has a couple of caving ladders along," Barrel said.

"He won't be able to go caving, will he?" Barry asked.

"If we take his ladder, he won't," was my reply.

Barrel was concerned. "I trust we won't find too many spots like the one we had on Ama Dablam. At that altitude, we're not going to get porters up any overhangs. How high do you anticipate Sherpas are going to have to carry, Tom?"

"To 27,500—Camp 6."

"Are the summit teams carrying only oxygen up there?" Barry asked.

"Yes," I said. "Thirty, thirty-five pounds, mostly oxygen. The others will be carrying thirty-five plus their oxygen bottle, making forty-eight pounds in all."

"That's a hell of a carry, isn't it?" Barrel asked.

"Yep. We decided we're going to have to hump ourselves on this route," Willi said.

"No guts, no glory," Barry added.

The problem of load carrying over such difficult terrain made it seem desirable to place our final camp below the steep rock step we could see on the skyline, rather than above it. "But I don't think you can hope that one assault party can climb that step and go clear to the top in one day." Barrel said.

"That's why there are two assault parties," I replied. "The first one might be sacrificed on that step."

"We've only got eight hours of oxygen," Dave said.

"You've also got to leave time to get back down to camp by dark," Barry said.

Willi thought back to a discussion during the approach: "Gombu told us, 'Possible one night out, Sahib. One night sleep out—no bags, no tent, move out next morning.'"

"Up or down?" Barry asked.

"He didn't specify," Willi answered. "I was afraid to ask."

"That's introducing a thought that I just don't like at all," said Barrel, half-smiling.

I replied, "If you don't lose too much fat, I won't mind bivouacing with you, Barrel."

"Well, I don't know if we'll ever come to that or not," Willi said. "But maybe so. Standards are certainly moving up in the Himalaya. People are treating the high terrain much more casually than they have before."

"It might be possible to survive the night, but I wonder how capable one would be the next day," Barrel said.

"I don't know that I'd like to bivouac too high up there," I said. "I'm not sure my few remaining brain cells could tolerate it too well."

"And if you had a wind . . ." Jake said.

"Yes," Willi said. "Gombu had another interesting observation. During good weather the wind blows from Tibet and creams the Col; but we'd be protected on the Ridge."

"Doesn't look that way from here," I replied. "And I would call this good weather. Looks like it's creaming the West Ridge."

"You're right,' Barrel added. "I've never seen the plume go in the other direction."

Willi continued. "During bad weather Gombu says it comes like this!" Vigorously he pantomimed a windstorm as only he could.

"It doesn't make any difference where you are in that case," I said, impressed by the intensity of his wind.

Jake brought up another problem: "A mile out on the North Face. That couloir's a hell of a long way off."

"But look where it goes," I replied. "Right to the top of the mountain."

"Hornbein always ignores the intervening steps in any route," Willi said.

"There's only one. That one right up there," I said, pointing to Everest's skyline, three miles above. Conversation stopped, as we stared. Then it was time for lunch.

* * *

After six days at Thyangboche, acclimatizing to the altitude and waiting for the snow to melt, we moved on toward the mountain on March 15. The walk began with a somewhat helter-skelter descent to the Imja Khola. Our new, unyielding Eiger boots skidded resolutely down the foot-pocked icy trail, totally in control of their wearers, who followed precariously after. The boots proved fairly comfortable in spite of their rocking chair inflexibility.

We enjoyed many and changing views of Ama Dablam as we passed around it to the West. Everest dwindled and finally disappeared behind the Nuptse Ridge, but other peaks rose spectacularly into view. The higher we went the colder it got, and there was even a nippiness in the sunshine whenever a slight breeze blew.

On the following day we climbed the terminal moraine of the Khumbu Glacier to Lobuje at 16,000 feet for the second phase of our acclimatization. Innumerable small peaks about us were tempting. Up-valley a portion of the West Shoulder peeked from behind the Nuptse buttress. The sun shining on that flat white crest stirred longings to be sitting up there looking at the mysteries still hidden. We sat about the breakfast table discussing the direction our acclimatization energies should take.

Norm started the discussion: "The weather is beautiful and I know lots of you are very eager to get started on the Icefall. You'd like to rush in there and immediately get up. Let me say right now, definitely not today. It's too early. We are far earlier than any previous Everest expedition. I would suggest this for today. Do some minor scrambles; whether you want to climb boulders or go up on this moraine, or whatever—picture taking —get used to the altitude. I'd like to find out how many of you would like to go up Lobuje Peak."

As I listened to the plans being made I became uneasy. My only previous experience in the Himalaya had left me imbued with the Nick Clinch philosophy that you have to make every day of reasonable weather count. Particularly if we were to spread ourselves over two routes, we would need all the time we could muster come the end of May. Unable to contain myself, I dove in.

"Can we start the discussion over and first determine the demands on personnel for moving a team straight into the Icefall?"

"There are no demands," Norman said, "because we are not going to move up to Base Camp tomorrow. I think Tom has been most outspoken about his eagerness to come to grips with the Icefall. If the Icefall has had much snow you can't do much good on it—you won't know where the best route is. Here's my suggestion, and this is based on the experience of two previous expeditions. When we get to Base Camp, we have a lot to do: set up the radio station, unpack everything, organize everything, get used to the altitude. Then, by all means, conditions permitting, we should get started. But let us not be hasty. Let's not rush like fools into the Icefall."

Committed now, I tried to explain. "Well, Norm, I hate to always be sounding as if I'm in a damned hurry, but I guess I am, possibly. It seems to me that we should be taking advantage, as long as we're feeling fit, of every day that we possibly can. I would frankly like to see a party move up on the 19th to Base Camp and start planning a route up the thing."

Norm replied, "Tom, there's only one thing. Those of you who are West Ridge bound, I can assure you, are going to have a nasty surprise when you get up on the West Shoulder, because of wind. If you get there too early, it's going to kill you. It may kill you to such an extent that you don't want to go on to the top."

Thinking back to Makalu in 1954, Will agreed, "I don't think you should ever underestimate the effect of the wind. It can knock you off faster than the altitude."

"Yes," I said, "but the only way to know about this is to actually bump into it head on, I'm afraid."

"Tom, I am the last man to be defeatist," Norm replied. "You will never find me defeatist. I'm just saying, I see no point, Tom, and I repeat it, for any of us to get into the Icefall before the 27th. Trust my judgment; I've been there twice. Don't overestimate yourself, Tom."

"I'm not. I know I'm damned weak, Norm. But still you don't know what the conditions are. You try them out and if the weather is good . . ."

Willi came to my rescue. "This is Tom's argument: that there is no question of beating ourselves to a frazzle on the Icefall, but it does seem reasonable to launch an early probe, in the orderly course of acclimatization and all, and find out the depth of snow. As you look at each other over the surface, you say, 'O.K. we wait a week.' But if it should be just that strange year that the route could be put in earlier, we'd be that much farther ahead."

"We are right now," Norm pointed out. "The way the plans are, we are twelve days earlier than the original plan and five days earlier than the revised plan."

"That's good," Willi said. "But let's be three days earlier than that."

"I just don't want to rush up there and right away kill ourselves sleeping too high," Norm said.

"I agree with you," I replied.

"It's interesting how we manage to generate some tension just

Narrative continues on page 112

. . . every sound was stilled, every light vanished, and a sudden wave of peace enveloped the wanderer. What a small space is occupied by human life in the vastness of the mountains!

The valley was all sunk in shadow, but an undefined glare appeared high up in the dark sky and attracted my gaze; all the highest peaks of the chain . . . were still glowing, glowing softly with a hidden flame, as if they were illuminated by an internal fire that did not shine through the stone. It was a calm, strong light, that made no shadows, that lit up no other part of the earth or the sky, but wrapped the peaks alone in a mantle of golden red, the red of old amber, the red of wavy hair, or of transparent leaves in the October sun: and the peaks seemed to shine alone in the colourless vault, and to hang as if they did not touch the earth; they were like unreal shapes, created from nothing, like phantoms that live by night in the terrible heights of the sky and only appear now and then to sleepers in their dreams.

I did not recognize the beautiful forms I had seen by day; they had increased beyond measure, they had changed their appearance, they no longer belonged to our world; they were shadows of other unknown mountains cast by an unexplained phenomenon on to our sky by some distant star.

—Guido Rey

GIL ROBERTS: Kangtega and evening clouds, from Pheriche

The true mountaineer is a wanderer, and by a wanderer I do not mean a man who expends his whole time in travelling to and fro in the mountains on the exact tracks of his predecessors . . . but I mean a man who loves to be where no human being has been before, who delights in gripping rocks that have previously never felt the touch of human fingers, or in hewing his way up ice-filled gullies whose grim shadows have been sacred to the mists and avalanches since "earth rose out of chaos." In other words, the true mountaineer is the man who attempts new ascents. Equally, whether he succeeds or fails, he delights in the fun and jollity of the struggle. The gaunt, bare slabs, the square, precipitous steps in the ridge, and the black, bulging ice of the gully, are the very breath of life to his being. I do not pretend to be able to analyse this feeling, still less to be able to make it clear to unbelievers. It must be felt to be understood, but it is potent to happiness and sends the blood tingling through the veins, destroying every trace of cynicism and striking at the very roots of pessimistic philosophy.

—A. F. MUMMERY

JAMES LESTER: *Boulder detail near Lobuje, and Nuptse*

in attitudes when the actual plans that either of us suggest would be identical," said Willi.

"I said it to individuals and I will say it to the whole group," Norm said. "When we had the meeting to talk about the acclimatization period, I was being a bit cagey about it. My original plan was always to move toward the Icefall as straight as possible. I personally have been here several times, but I know a lot of the younger climbers wanted to try some first ascents. When the consensus came, I found everybody wanted the same. I couldn't have been more delighted, but I didn't want to be dictatorial, saying, 'We're going to go straight into the Icefall.' "

Noddy, Captain Prabakher Shumshere Jung Bahadur Rana, our small silent Nepalese liaison officer, sat listening, a little awed by the malleability that characterized democratic decision making. A few days later at Gorak Shep he was even more perplexed by the final turn of events. The Icefall recon group moved up to Base with Norman in the lead, and that same day Barry and I headed off on a two-day climbing lark on an appealing rock pinnacle.

* * *

Going from Gorak Shep to Base was like passing into still another world. Below there was natural shelter and a gentleness of tundra-covered moraine to offset the surrounding harshness. Passing through the towering ice pinnacles of Phantom Alley we entered the rock-strewn valley floor at the bottom of a huge amphitheater. The end of the valley was enclosed by the dark rock walls of Pumori, Lingtren, and Khumbutse. From hanging glaciers ice would periodically calve, rolling valleyward like beautiful, short-lived waterfalls. From Lobuje we had been unable to detect the faintest hint of an access to the upper reaches of Everest but now it was there to see. Squeezed between Nuptse and the West Shoulder, the Icefall plunged in crumbling confusion from the mouth of the Cwm to the valley floor two thousand feet below. Here it turned sharply, to flow southward as the Khumbu Glacier. We set up our Base Camp at 17,800 feet on the lateral moraine that formed the outer edge of the turn. Huge boulders lent an air of solidarity to the place, but the rolling rubble underfoot corrected the misimpression. All that one could see and feel and hear—of Icefall, moraine, avalanche, cold—was of a world not intended for human habitation. No water flowed, nothing grew—only destruction and decay.

Yet, as the red tents sprang up on carefully constructed platforms of rock, Base Camp slowly acquired a feeling of warmth. Al Auten's radio antenna linked us each evening with the outside world. Paths were cleared and bordered with rocks connecting the large living and mess tent with our satellite bedrooms. Within the large umbrella tent we placed our sagging table and folding chairs, the short-wave radio, Gil's dispensary, and Jim Ullman's carefully selected library. This would be home for the next several months, until the mountain was climbed.

. . . I imagined Paccard, Balmat, de Saussure and the others returning by this spot after having climbed the mountain of their dreams, and I said to myself: "Little men, face to face with the Accursed Mountain, they were not without courage. They were the first of the family of mountaineers, the foundations of the house."

And I said to myself again: "To them we owe the happiness of our youth. They have supported us in time of trouble, as yesterday, when their message 'What one man has done another can do' gave us strength. We may have done harder climbs than they, we may have explored remoter ranges, but it has been thanks to them; they showed us the way.

"Our climbs and bivouacs spent sagging from pitons in the great North faces, our terrible nights passed standing in two stirrups of cord, as on the Grand Capucin du Tacul, or at the bottom of a crevasse as on Annapurna are analogous to the first attempts and bivouacs of Jacques Balmat when there were no huts on the mountain; our Himalayan camps are the brothers of Whymper's camps on the ridges of the Matterhorn."

"Where there's a will there's a way" was as much the rule for de Saussure sweating under his perruque as for Mummery conquering the Grépon, as much for Comici caparisoned with pitons and étriers in the north face of the Cima Grande di Laveredo as for Hillary and Tenzing scaling the roof of the world, all of them only stopping, like Regnard on his journey through Lapland, "where the earth went no further."

The alpinist dressed in silk and protected by face-veils has been succeeded by the Himalayan monster, disguised beneath a mask, loaded with oxygen bottles. But inside his different shell, man has not changed. We are of the same blood.

—Gaston Rebuffat

7. Jake

WE ESTABLISHED Base Camp on March 21 at 17,800 feet. On March 22 Willi, Big Jim, Lute, and Gombu entered the Icefall. The route went well. "This morning, the 23d," I wrote in my diary, "Barry, Dick, and I climbed the old moraine above camp to look with binoculars, first at our footsteps up the snow portions of the pinnacle Barry and I had climbed the day before, then at the five tiny figures moving into the Icefall two miles away. They seemed terribly inconsequential in the tumbling vastness. Finally up at the summit of Everest, the West Ridge shingling down in smooth, yellow strata in a most uninviting, but grossly foreshortened and misleading (I hope) manner. We lay in the sun gazing upward at the highest point on earth, clear against a blue sky, no plume of snow in evidence for a change. Almost dozing, feeling the pleasant weariness and fatigue of yesterday's exertions. Finally down to lunch, polishing our boots, which were a bit denuded of leather after yesterday's efforts. Now think I'll succumb to the delights of a horizontal position as my eyes won't stay open.

"3:45 P.M., still the 23d but 15 minutes later: a bit of suspense as Prather, surveying on the moraine, saw an avalanche come off the Lho La just beyond Base."

I picked up the walkie-talkie, climbed up toward him, and called Al Auten at Base.

"Yes, we saw the avalanche" he answered. "No one in that area at the time. But there may be an accident in the Icefall. Heard some shouts. Only see four coming down. Give us a call later."

Forty-five minutes later the voice came from the little box again: "There's been an accident. An icewall collapsed. A Sherpa's hurt. Jake's probably dead. A party's heading up there now."

Barry, Jake's closest friend, stood beside me, listening. The words sank sickeningly upon us both. Little more information came that evening from Base and we went to bed tearfully, hoping that there must be some mistake. Maybe Jake was hurt; he couldn't be dead.

The next day, a dull, snowy, chilly, cloud-shrouded day, there was no longer much doubt, just a soul-numbing acceptance of a tragic change in the way things had been. We plodded with this burden for two hours up the Khumbu among towering *névé penitentes* to Base and there gathered silently, greeted sadly by those who had been ahead. They told us the story.

Five of them had headed up to improve the route into the Icefall. At the time Dick Pownall, Ang Pema, and Jake were ahead on one rope. Ila Tsering and Gil Roberts had dropped back so Gil could clean his fogging goggles. Suddenly there was a muffled, groaning explosion, the ground heaved, and they were thrown downward. Gil and Ila were unhurt. Ahead the terrain was altered beyond recognition, a shattered chaos. A wall of ice "the size of two box cars, one atop the other" had collapsed. Pownall was half-buried, dazed but not seriously

hurt. Ang Pema was found a short distance back along the rope, frightened, his face badly cut. Three feet beyond him the rope disappeared beneath the collapsed wall. Jake was buried beneath tons of ice. He must have been killed instantly.

Gil's shouts were heard at Base. Unable to establish radio contact, and knowing that Jake had been carrying the radio, they sensed the disaster. A party started up. When they met the descending four, Big Jim put Ang Pema on his back and headed down while Willi and Lute continued on. They found the cut end of the rope vanishing into the ice. Willi climbed down into the cracks, shouting into the glacier. The only answer was the echo of his own voice. Still, as the light faded, it was hard to leave. Obvious though the answer seemed, doubt lingered.

My diary continues: "As we sit here at Base, looking straight into the jaws of the Icefall, we all feel the deep, abiding presence of one of us up there, and all ponder the justice and luck, or the lack of it. But now we all realize the need, for more than Jake's sake, to go on up and finish our, and his, climb."

For Dick Pownall this was something new. He was a powerful, confident rock climber, accustomed to maintaining complete control of his environment. Never in all those years of guiding had he seen an accident. Now a mountain had moved; unfeelingly, it had moved. Jake was dead. It could just as well have been him; for all his considerable strength and skill, survival on this mountain depended upon chance. Man was at the mercy of his environment. It wasn't an easy lesson to learn. We could see his shock and wondered when he would come out of it and resume his interest in climbing.

I wrote in my diary about how impressively Barry went through the episode and how we talked late that night in our tent about Jake, Barry, and their ten years of rather parallel, yet dissimilar, existence. Jake was a quiet and sensitive individual. As both Barry and Willi put it, he had lost many battles. He escaped to the mountains, sought solace in them, and loved them. This expedition was the greatest event of his life. Barry had never seen Jake happier and more contented than in the last few weeks as we approached the mountain. Could knowing that he belonged in the mountains, knowing that away from them his life was largely an unsatisfied search for meaning, make his death more acceptable? Maybe it made it easier; I wasn't sure. At least this was how we rationalized Jake's death. We tried to make sensible something that had no sense, but inside it didn't help much.

In my diary, two days later, I recorded the surprise I felt about my own reactions and the rapidity of their transformation to the point where I could resume totally functional, if not totally enthusiastic, activity. I suppose this was wrought mostly by necessity to keep going, but it was strange how in some ways my feelings toward our undertaking were so little altered by Jake's death. The first shock brought forth the question: If this is mountaineering, is it worth it? Then answers

came: Mountaineering is not the sacrifice of life. We climb, deluding ourselves that death cannot happen to us if we carefully appraise hazards, techniques, and the nature of mountains. Of course climbing is not absolutely safe, and we accept risk when we climb, making it a seemingly reasonable, justifiable part of the challenge. Therefore, one cannot regret being there when a death occurs, as it occasionally must. One must just go on, thankful for being spared—or quit.

We still had to climb the mountain, for too many reasons—most simply and materially because there was too much invested, too much at stake for the entire expedition to turn around and return home at this point. It was simply impossible. But this was a miserable justification on which to continue. How could one put in the day-to-day effort, face the hazards and discomforts only because there was an obligation to someone or something that endowed the expedition? Fortunately, there was no question of this. All felt the strong need, the desire, to go on, not only for Jake, but also for each of us individually and as a group. There was no change in this.

But there were changes. Some, like Pownall, lived alone with their thoughts, fighting their battle silently. Others articulated it: "I'll go through the Icefall twice," Gil Roberts declared, "—once up and once down." Inevitably, the question of the West Ridge arose. How could we justify the added risk? Or could we? We all had doubts. Barrel expressed his to Dave and Gil one afternoon. Were there others who thought it an unjustifiable luxury? Gil suggested to Willi that he bring it up for discussion, which Willi did that evening after dinner:

"We had a suggestion made today that we have a group discussion concerning the double route that was previously proposed—that we may be too weak now to consider it. We are weaker than merely by the loss of a man. There have been scars left on different members of us that could influence future performance, and the suggestion was presented with enough strength that I thought it was at least wise to discuss. I don't know how deep you want to go into it. Does anyone have a suggestion or observation?"

Will Siri was puzzled. "What specifically are you referring to right now?"

"The launching of any attempt at the West Ridge," Willi answered.

"This is presuming that the reconnaissance will nonetheless go on, right?" Gil asked.

"Well, I'm not even sure of that, not necessarily," Willi replied. "What it amounts to is this: I think it's a feeling that we've all had, at least I know it was certainly mine, that immediately after Jake's death we just wanted to finish with this mountain and get out. Wanted to get off the darn thing as fast as possible, and the fastest way is to pour everything we have into the Col, climb it, and go home. This, I think is the

major feeling involved and I know some of us still feel this very keenly. The question is whether it's worth trying the West Ridge or not, in the light of the present circumstances and the further practical question whether we have a ghost of a chance to pull off both routes now. That's the nub of the matter."

Gil persisted. "Well, it would seem to me that whether we have a ghost of a chance or not, it's still a worthwhile mountaineering objective for reconnoitering."

Will approached the question from a slightly different point of view. "As I recall the discussions we had back in the States and in Kathmandu, I think we all felt at that time that the major drive would be to the South Col—this gave the greatest assurance of putting a team on the summit. And there would be a reconnaissance of the Shoulder. From Kathmandu to here, there was a growing feeling and a growing enthusiasm for the West Ridge. More and more emphasis was put on this, understandably, and finally it became an equal operation. I think we've got to recognize the turn of events. Perhaps the larger effort should be put on the South Col with a reasonable reconnaissance on the West Shoulder. And if things go well there, then the decision can be revised."

"It seems to me that a decision on the West Ridge is a little premature," Barry said. "For two reasons actually: we don't know what the hell we're talking about up there, and I think I, at least, am experiencing the return of the desire to climb."

Barry's closeness to Jake lent special significance to his words. If others had doubts about climbing the West Ridge, they were left unsaid.

As Expedition leader, Norman must have felt somehow responsible for Jake's death. It would have been easy to play the game conservatively, but he understood the team better than many understood themselves at this particular moment.

"I hope I haven't misjudged the caliber of the team," he began, then stated that unless he missed his guess most of us would like to continue as we had originally planned.

One question remained. Could it still be fun, or had this tragedy so altered the morale, the feeling, the pleasure of the Expedition that it could not be recaptured?

After a snowy day's hard work on equipment at Base, it became apparent that the spirit of us all, Jake's spirit too, since it was part of us, and also part of the mountain we wished to climb, sustained itself in us. It was inevitable that tomorrow or the next day, or the next, each of us must pay tribute by passing directly over Jake's grave. With this obstacle behind and no longer a hazard, we must climb the mountain with as much as we could retrieve of the spirit and joy we had when we started, that spirit and joy which for Jake were perhaps the greatest he had ever known.

THOMAS HORNBEIN: Snow banners above Khumbu Icefall

8. Icefall

WITH ROPE, ladder, and bridge we finally tamed the Icefall but never felt we had achieved more than a precarious truce. On each journey through the chaos of ice, past the blue-green crevasses, and over the tumbled blocks that marked the grave, we heard the groans of a glacier stretched on a rack of granite, the *whoompf* as a block subsided underfoot, and the rumble as towers collapsed and spilled tons of ice. The place was rotting, piece by piece. Pausing to rest, I could relax completely, yet never quite dispel the feeling that I was an uninvited guest.

An aluminum ladder spanned a deep gash near the top, leaning swaybacked against the wall on the other side. On April 2, Pownall, Dick, and I were preparing to descend from Camp 1 to sculpt the upper part of this wall into a form more reassuring to laden porters. For some reason Pownall asked for a delay. Twenty minutes later, as we stood outside our tents roping up, the mountain started coming apart. The rolling boom drew our eyes to the chaotic dissolution of the icy canyon just below. Two hundred yards away, towers began to topple, walls sagged into rubble. In a chain reaction, the gigantic breaker curled toward us. I stood transfixed, unconsciously bracing myself against the moment our camp should become part of it. Thick clouds rose from the cauldron, ice particles shimmering like tiny diamonds before the hidden sun, then settling as dust upon our camp. When the air had cleared, the camp had not moved.

Pownall was visibly shaken. But for his delay we would be buried under the ruins of the route. For him this was too familiar, striking notes of fear and then perplexity at the fate that had spared him for the second time; it was enough for one day. "This Icefall is much too busy," I wrote. "I am not at all sad to be above and beyond the Monster."

On March 31 Dick, Willi, and I had moved up from Base to Camp 1. I only made it half way: "Dump Camp, 19,300. Here I sit like a stupid idiot. 7:30 P.M., alone in a 2-man Drawtite tent with a gastrointestinal tract behaving a mite like Vesuvius. About 11:30 Dick and I started up toward Camp 1, rather too heavily laden, I suspect, but carrying all necessary clothing for our journey to the West Shoulder. We went slowly but fairly well. Abominably hot. Towers capsizing audibly, and once visibly, on either side in the heat of the afternoon. But the route itself seems pretty good with very few suspicious-looking exceptions. We stopped for a drink and some Tobler chocolate, then on to the dump. Shortly my stomach began to react with intermittent cramps. As we came closer to the dump, pains came closer, nearly doubling me. We finally crept into camp, spotting Willi waiting (he had left an hour earlier, alone, with nearly 80 pounds instead of 60; still

made it in 2¾ hours instead of our 3½). I flipped out of my pack and rushed down the hill. Finally I crept into the tent in chilled discomfort to appraise my condition. Each exertion brought new spasms. I decided to stay here. Willi and Dick left me their water bottles and headed up about 4 P.M. The next hour or so I spent in intermittent agonies, trying to create a space in the tent to sleep, bring in food boxes, inflate air mattress, get myself and precious water into the sleeping bag since with no stove burner here I dare not let it freeze. The ordeal was slow, punctuated at 2–4 minute intervals by return of cramps with each exertion, so I had to lie back and rest about three-fourths of the time. Finally the job was somewhat done, even my pack was hauled in from the outside. I got in my bag and dozed till shortly before 6, then scooted to the door for radio contact, hearing Jim and Al conversing but unable to get through. I learned that Prather and Tashi were coming down from Camp 1 and there goes my night of lonely isolation that I had hoped to be recovered enough to enjoy. There are compensations, though, in the feeling of security. I don't aim to go down, plan to keep pushing toward the West Ridge recon which, frankly, is the thing I have dreamt most of and which threatens to be the most exciting portion of the expedition, except perhaps reaching the summit by the same route. So somehow my intestinal tract is going to have to shape up in the next two days whether it likes it or not."

The next morning I was totally purged and boomed up to Camp 1 with Tashi carrying half my load. I seemed to be going as strongly as any but the incredible Unsoeld, who appeared to have gone maniacally awry, threatening to demoralize the Expedition by his extreme hyper-activity, hyper-optimism, and seeming indestructibility.

I was puzzled. What was Willi trying to prove? Soloing half the Icefall unroped and beneath an 80-pound load, for example? Was this his way of leading us all back into the fray again after Jake's death? If so, it must be lonely out there in the front, shouting *"Charge!"* to a contingent out of earshot. The effort told even on him, for he climbed weary and aching into his sleeping bag each night. And it wasn't quite achieving the desired results. Most of us didn't need such a boost. Some were more cowed than invigorated by Willi's energy, asking themselves, "How can we hope to keep up with that?" Finally, Dick and I hauled him aside:

"Slow down, Willi, you're demoralizing half the Expedition."

"Don't be ridiculous; I've been holding back so you youngsters can keep up with me."

But the thought had been planted and it grew; Willi slowed.

9. Reconnaissance

ON APRIL 3 Dick and I slogged up the Cwm to set up housekeeping at Advance Base. The long, gradual stroll seemed interminable as we wandered back and forth between crevasses. We paused often to sit on our packs and nibble a bit of fruitcake, and to look at the tiny figures of the Sherpas far ahead.

"God, the camp must be another couple of miles," Dick said. "I don't think we'll ever get there."

Inside, I wearily agreed, but I couldn't let Dick get discouraged. "No, it's just over that rise, below those ice cliffs where the Swiss had theirs." I willed the camp to be there.

It seemed almost too familiar after all the pictures. Familiar, except for the scale of things: Everest, bulking huge above the West Shoulder, Lhotse, foreshortened at the head of the Cwm, the wall of Nuptse soaring a vertical mile above our heads, its glassy slabs of ice shimmering in the sunlight. The Valley of Silence, up which we plodded, appeared almost level, but our labor belied the illusion. Heat, reflected from the surrounding walls, converged at the valley floor. I felt trapped in a gigantic reflector oven. My mind sought some distraction—a poem, plans for the West Ridge, thoughts of home—but heat drove thought away. I found myself counting steps. One foot, then another. Ten steps, and a drop of sweat dripped from the end of my nose; another ten, nope, only made nine before the next drip dropped—drop dripped? Try for ten. Nine again, dammit. Is Emerson talking to himself up there? He must be completely fuzzed by the altitude. But still, where does he get the wind to talk? All mine's used up just breathing.

Not till the homeward journey did Dick confess that he wasn't talking to himself but to the tape recorder hidden in his vest. His demeanor, though not an act, was nevertheless designed to test the nature of my response, which, committed to tape, became a part of his sociological study.

At 21,350 feet, midway up the Cwm, Advance Base was higher than any point on the North American continent. This was the jumping-off point for the two routes. From here we would go up-Cwm to the base of the Lhotse Face and the South Col, or would take "the one less traveled by." We could look straight up to the point where the West Shoulder bumped against the mountain itself, against the West Ridge.

According to plan the reconnaissance of the West Ridge would have first priority once Advance Base was established. The equipment for the recon accumulated there slowly, since we had temporarily outrun our line of supply.

"One big problem," I wrote home, "has been with our Sherpas. Perhaps it is the big, fat, rich American image, and the fact that they have been at this too many years, but it is much like a labor union trying to put on the squeeze. It began four or five days ago at Base when they requested a second sleeping bag (the Indians had supplied two kapok bags last year). Instead of saying flatly no, that one Bauer bag was adequate (which it is), we agreed to pay them 25 rupees a month.

"Next we get to Camp 1 to discover that many of the loads coming up are 35–40 pounds, not the 50 planned for, and we cannot get our Sherpas to carry full 50-pound loads to Advance Base. This all adds up to more carries, loss of time, and a diminution in chances of success, at least on the West Ridge, if not the Col. Willi tried to put four oxygen bottles (52 pounds) on one man to Advance Base but was forced to compromise because of new snow (3 inches) and a 'difficult track, Sahib.' The next day I fell heir to the job and went through the same nonsense ('difficult balance on log bridges with heavy load, Sahib') but finally got a carry up here that approached 50 pounds per man, with much grumbling and unhappiness on the part of all, especially me, for I find such a role not delectable."

We sat at Advance Base, forced into a one- or two-day delay in starting the recon. I hovered protectively over the pile growing slowly outside the mess tent, taking repeated inventories—pickets, ice screws, fixed rope, one four-man tent, and twelve oxygen bottles—and mentally figuring deficits. All we needed were the stoves and three food boxes. Big Jim, Lute, and Dick Pownall eyed those forbidden goods enviously. As the pile grew, so did their discontent, a discontent derived from impatience to begin the buildup of the Lhotse Face, and nurtured by the oblivious enthusiasm with which I sequestered the incoming supplies. This was the first sign of a conflict that was inevitable between the two routes. From now on we would be competing for manpower and equipment to accomplish our separate goals.

The basis for conflict could be sensed long before, almost with the first separation into two teams. The growing enthusiasm of one team for its route heightened awareness in the other of the competition necessary to fulfill its own needs. As a result opinions were stated more forcefully—and less charitably—than they were felt. Thus the original separation born of personal desire was accentuated by an interaction in which each team found the other increasingly more vigorous and dogmatic in its own defense. The thing that saved it was that usually we were aware we overstated our cases. Though in group discussion I might be outspoken in defense of the West Ridge, in the privacy of my tent I could readily admit my understanding of the South Colers' point of view and express my doubts about the West Ridge. Others must have faced the same problem of achieving compatibility between their goals and that which they knew was just. The value and rightness of one route over another was solely a matter of where each man's hopes and ambitions lay. To avoid conflict was impossible. How constructively such conflict might be resolved would depend on the maturity and self-control of the individuals involved, and on their ability to compromise.

At Thyangboche we had chosen the team of four for the recon; now Dick was not to be a part of it. Each meal he ate refused to stay down. Weak simply from lack of food, he headed dejectedly down to Base to recover. From my own

intense anticipation of the coming adventure I could imagine his disappointment. Jake's death left Barry or Dave, who were at Camp 1, to fill the empty hole.

"Who will it be, Willi?"

"Dave. Neither of them is feeling too well at the moment. I'd rather save Barry for the build-up. I have the feeling we'd be better off using Dave early since I'm not sure how enthusiastic he is for the Ridge since Jake's death."

Dave came up from Camp 1, not overjoyed at having to climb while feeling so poorly. On the following day, April 7, Barrel, our seven Sherpas, and I headed up to establish camp at the dump site. Dave would rest the day at Advance Base and come up with Willi early the next morning. It was a blustery day, and windswept snow scoured the Cwm. Even old Tashi wanted to turn back at the bottom of the fixed rope, but we were too close to the Dump.

"Just a couple of miles more, Tashi," I said, and his eyes lit as he heard the Sherpa answer to our own frequent questions during the approach march.

Willi and Dave showed up on schedule. Unfortunately, starting at 6 A.M., they had encountered not only wind, but also the bitterness of early morning cold. When they poured puffing into the tent, Willi's hands were beyond his feeling them, but their effect on my bare stomach was something else again. Dave was just plain tired. Our plan had been to push on to the Shoulder to establish camp and begin the Reconnaissance, but it seemed like doubtful weather for climbing. As things developed the decision was not for us to make. From the kitchen, which was in the Sherpa tent, no sound emanated. It was after ten when Tashi appeared with morning tea.

"Passang Temba headache, Sahib," he reported. Caused by the rattling of wind-whipped tent?

Another hour and it was obvious that we had been stalemated. Had wind and Sahib ambition permitted, there were not enough daylight hours remaining for a carry to the Ridge. We sent the Sherpas down to Advance Base to save food. They would return empty in the morning to make the carry, weather permitting. Otherwise, we'd come down. We also resolved to keep possession of our own kitchen in the future. The rest of the day we ate peanut butter and talked.

April 9 was clear and calm. The seven Sherpas pulled in just as Willi and I started breaking the trail toward the fixed ropes. Once around the icy corner we were in the open, switchbacking up steep slopes. The snow was firm, occasionally icy. At least none of that knee-to-waist-deep stuff we had labored through on Masherbrum—one fringe benefit of Everest winds. Willi's feet flailed steps in the snow as he steamed ahead. Coming behind on the rope was breathtaking. Each change of direction required fresh gymnastics, flipping the rope, collecting coils, running to turn the corners, then gasping for air as Willi moved steadily forward.

"Dammit, Willi, what are you trying to do?"

He smiled back, thought for a moment, and replied, "Just testing you."

"For what?"

"Bigger things."

When the snow is hard and crampons grip well, it is easier to go first than second. You can move at a continuous pace, zigzagging up the slope, while your companion, forced to keep the slack out of the rope, follows erratically after. Willi was going all out, and the figures of the others dwindled below, but after a time it became easier to hold the pace. Finally, as we neared 23,000 feet, Willi stopped, panting.

"Let's trade off for awhile."

Now Willi suffered the inconvenience of coming second; the rope became taut behind as we proceeded. With almost impersonal detachment I observed this stretching of my limits, filing the information away for the future and reveling in the pleasure of the effort.

By 4 P.M. we were still below the West Shoulder, which was hidden by falling snow. The late hour, weariness, and sheer boredom with putting one foot in front of the other all encouraged a decision to stop. Our search for a tent platform was frustrated by the flat light that made it impossible to gauge the angle of the slope. We dumped our loads below the bergschrund and began hacking out a tent platform. Dave and Barrel arrived, slipped out of their packs and sat down on top of them. We thanked the Sherpas, promising them a day's rest for their truly long hard carry, a promise that added to the impatience of the South Colers. With only a couple of hours of light remaining, the Sherpas hurriedly departed for Advance Base. Our four-man tent was soon erected. Four people with gear could barely be accommodated crosswise. Cooking would have to be done in the vestibule. I chose the spot nearest the kitchen, determined that we should fare better than on the deadly diet of Pong. As I unleashed my latent culinary creativity, the old guide sat back enjoying the unaccustomed luxury of being waited on.

Stuffed with curried-ketchup-covered shrimp and rice, we prepared for sleep. Dutifully filling in our diaries, another part of Emerson's sociological study, I came to the line beginning, "Tomorrow, if possible, I should; will; would like to—" I scratched the last two choices and filled in the blank, "Tomorrow, if possible, I *will* survey the first step."

Now, at 23,800 feet we were to sample the benefits of sleeping oxygen. Feeling exceedingly healthy after our race, Willi and I viewed the use of oxygen more as a game than a useful necessity. Still there was pleasure in the status symbol, for now we were joining the Big League as high-altitude Everesters. Add curiosity, the challenge of a new experience, and the realization that ultimately it would make a difference, and we were hooked. For me, too, there was the question of how all the gear I had labored so long over was going to work.

Two yellow cylinders were hauled inside, like fish from the frozen sea—one for Dave and Barrel, one for Willi and me. I explained their use with an aura of confidence to conceal that I had never slept on oxygen before, either. A liter per minute oxygen flow was split by a plastic T to be shared by two, reminiscent of a fine old Cole Porter song. Barry and Dave slid into their polyethylene sleeping masks and with disgusting ease were soon asleep. Meanwhile, Willi and I lay awake savoring the new sensation.

"It's kind of warm inside this thing, Willi."

"Yes; I'm suffocating," he replied, ripping the mask off, gasping for air.

"I think I could swim in mine, but the darn thing's overflowing into my sleeping bag."

Finally we achieved some sense of satisfaction by dispensing with the mask and holding the end of the hose beneath our noses, sniffing oxygen and trusting some unconscious instinct to hold the proper relation between hose and nose as we slept. I dozed, then awoke, searching for the end of the hose in the innards of my well-oxygenated sleeping bag. Enough of that. I plugged my climbing mask into the T. That mask would be comfortable. But sleep didn't come. No oxygen. The flow-indicator on the mask delivery tube provided enough resistance to shunt the entire supply to Willi, who was now sleeping peacefully with the hose jammed delicately into one nostril. Then a sudden surge of gas as Willi's nose plugged up and I acquired the total flow. I slept, he woke, and so it went for several nights until we finally made our peace with the plastic aquariums. Eventually they provided all the psychological security and womblike warmth any foetus could desire.

The dewy night was followed by an even dewier awakening. As the sun hit the tent, the frost which had condensed on the inner liner began to liquefy. We could lie in our bags watching the drops form and creep to the center of the flat roof top. From the growing pool rain began to fall on the captive audience below.

The effort of cooking and dressing is breathlessly exhausting at high altitude, and even the simplest task is terribly time consuming. But that first day we set a new record—it took us five hours, not owing to altitude so much as just plain chaos. I had wakened to find myself shoved into the vestibule, wrapped cozily around a can of peanut butter. The place looked as if it had been stirred by a power mixer. The four of us were just the beginning. Air mattresses, sleeping bags, oxygen bottles, down parkas, anoraks, reindeer boots, overboots, diaries, first-aid kits, radio, were all well mixed. I hung in the vestibule, brewing soup, while the others tried to dodge the interior monsoon.

"Has anyone seen my other rag sock?"

"No, that one's mine—I think."

Once shod, we emerged into the white open spaces to rope up—Willi and Dave, Barrel and I. That went all right. Crampons on, then oxygen. We'd be using it for climbing from here up. It was strange and new; screwing in regulators, hooking on delivery tubes, valves open, flow at two liters per minute.

Finally at noon we were off into the fog, headed toward the crest of the West Shoulder for the long-anticipated view. Here there was no question that oxygen made a difference; climbing was a delight. There was a little extra spring in the step, a reserve of energy and alertness to meet the unexpected. Best of all there was freedom to think about more than the alternate plod-pant-plod, with ten breaths per plod; there was freedom to enjoy the view, and to have thoughts to be alone with.

I was very much aware of the rubber mask on my face because I had designed it. On Masherbrum our single attempt to use oxygen ended because of the effort required to breath through the masks. That same summer Gombu and two Indian companions were turned back high on Everest when they couldn't remove ice that had formed on the breathing valves of similar sets. The same type of mask had got the British and Swiss to the top of Everest, but in ideal weather. The idea for a far simpler and more reliable mask took shape in my mind during my research on respiration. Fred Maytag's enthusiasm brought it to reality. His company was more accustomed to manufacturing washing machines than high-altitude oxygen masks, but members of the research division spent many extra hours creating a mold which permitted the entire unit to be made as a single piece of rubber. The result was a mask with one valve instead of six. It could be de-iced by simply squeezing the rubber breathing cone with a mittened hand. Though climbing was one adventure Fred Maytag had not tasted, he understood it and enjoyed being part of our undertaking. He died of cancer three months before the expedition departed.

His mask fit comfortably, even around a nose like mine; the goggles didn't fog from my breath. I watched the oxygen bladder expand and contract with each breath, fascinated by its motion. I consciously overbreathed to accentuate the movement.

Suddenly, I felt the rope come tight as Barrel shouted breathlessly: "Slow down, Tom!" He was having trouble getting synchronized with his oxygen. In my fascination with the equipment, my pace had increased considerably, gradually narrowing the gap to Willi and Dave, who had started earlier. Willi, looking back, saw us coming.

"Aha," he thought. "Hornbein's trying to beat me to the Shoulder." He brought Dave up to him. "Let me check your flow, Dave," he said, unobtrusively turning Dave's regulator to a full flow of four liters per minute, and off they went.

Unaware of the competition I had provoked, I paused and brought Barrel up to me. After checking his oxygen equipment, I suggested that he set the pace. Ahead, Willi's feet flailed like piledrivers into the snow. The gap between the two ropes steadily widened. What drive, I thought, but what's his hurry? What's he trying to prove and who to? I'd never climbed with anyone so intensely competitive. I wondered if the competition was more than just a game, how much it accounted for his tireless drive, his choice of route.

As essentially a noncompetitor myself, I could not say. Yet I was lured into the simple childlike fun of the game. Could I keep up with Unsoeld, whose power on Masherbrum I too well recalled? I thought back to the day nearly three years before when I was toiling uphill at 23,000 feet, heavily laden. Willi, starting an hour later had steamed past me under the burden of a huge army rucksack.

"Can I take your pack, Tom?" he had shouted from fifty yards ahead.

"No thanks, Willi," I had answered, sagging to the snow, "I'll die first."

The game he lured me into now was rather ridiculous, as Dick pointed out later, when Willi, with unnecessary relish, described how we had tried to run each other into the ground. Though the game could tell me I might have the steam to keep up with him, it left untouched the more basic question of my relationship with the mountain and myself.

Willi and Dave were sitting nonchalantly on their packs staring into blank nothingness when Barrel and I joined them. For the next three hours we all sat transfixed, as the mists played

AL AUTEN: In Camp 2, Hornbein, Corbet, Emerson
RICHARD M. EMERSON: Hornbein and Martian

ethereal games, parting to reveal tantalizing glimpses of what we had come to see. All around us was a confusion of vignettes as momentary rifts in the curtain unveiled the dim outline of the North Col, or of improbable bastions, belonging presumably to the West Ridge, or of rock floating free, fantastically high above. During the course of the afternoon, we must have glimpsed most of it, but only piece-meal, as isolated bits of a puzzle which seemed fearsomely greater than the sum of all its parts—a jumble of black, snow-etched walls and arêtes that ended nowhere.

After waiting in vain for the unveiling of all we'd long anticipated in our dreams, we returned at four, chilled and snowed-upon, to the chaos of our tent. There was little to cheer about but a lot to anticipate. If only the mountain could be divested of its modesty. A reconnaissance is a hard chore to perform if you can't see anything. Not deterred by our lack of success, I closed my diary that day with: "Tomorrow, if possible, I *will* go above the first step."

On the 11th we got away an hour earlier. At the Shoulder the mountain waited, fully assembled. The cloud cauldron of the great South Face boiled, accentuating the black, twisting harshness of the West Ridge. We stared. Yesterday's fragments had not exaggerated. Our eyes climbed a mile of sloping, sedimentary shingles, black rock, yellow rock, gray rock, to the summit. The North Col was a thousand feet below us across this vast glacial amphitheater. As we stood where man had never stood before, we could look back into history. All the British attempts of the 'twenties and 'thirties had approached from the Rongbuk Glacier, over that Col, onto that North Face. The Great Couloir, Norton, Smythe, Shipton, Wager, Harris, Odell, our boyhood heroes. And there against the sky along the North Ridge, Mallory's steps. Everest was his more than any other man's. In 1924, as he approached the mountain from which he was not to descend, he had written: "Still the conquest of the mountain is the great thing, and the whole plan is mine and my part will be a sufficiently interesting one and will give me, perhaps, the best chance of all of getting to the top. It is almost unthinkable with this plan that I shan't get to the top; I can't see myself coming down defeated." This was the legacy we now looked upon. Our Ridge looked formidable. Once again the fear was there, and with the fear, the challenge: but *how*?

"That must be Hornbein's Couloir over there," Barrel said.

"You're right. I think it is," I replied.

"It's a long way over, Tom," said Willi.

"It sure is," I said. "I'm not even sure how to get into it unless we can traverse from here."

"How about that crack diagonally up through the cliff, just left of where the Shoulder meets the Ridge?" Dave asked.

"Yes, that looks possible," Willi agreed. "From there we can either cross to Hornbein's Couloir, if we have to, or cut back up Jake's to gain the West Ridge above the first step."

"Sounds reasonable," I said. "But those cliffs overhanging Jake's Couloir don't look too inviting."

"Not without a lot of preparation," Willi said. "But it's an awful lot closer than that avalanche gully of yours. That's a couple of miles over there and we're not even sure it cuts through the Yellow Band."

"I don't see any signs of avalanche from it, though," I replied.

"No, but just wait till it snows," Willi said.

The plan was for Willi and me to try to reach Hornbein's Couloir. Barry and Dave would tackle the Ridge itself, nearer, but less appetizing. We headed out, following the corniced edge. Finally, where the cornice faded, we stepped across into Tibet. As we climbed, the cauldron overflowed and once again the mountain was lost in cloud. At 24,500 feet we nibbled a bit of frozen tuna and fruitcake, waiting in vain for some hint of our objective. Toward three we turned back, picking up Dave and Barrel on the way.

It was hardly a cheerful evening. The two days of reconnaissance originally planned were gone. Our hope had been to surmount the first step, but thus far we hadn't even reached the base of the Ridge. This side of the mountain could be climbed by a well-equipped, full-scale attempt; chances for a small offshoot of the major effort seemed pretty slim. For Sherpas to carry loads over that rock would require days of route preparation with fixed ropes and ladders. It seemed hopeless.

Dave was for going down in the morning. "We shouldn't burn ourselves out here for nothing," he said. "They can use us on the Col." The logic was sound, except that there were too many people on the Col already. Willi, Barrel, and I felt a gnawing doubt. How much might the weather and our poor acclimatization be influencing our judgment? We hadn't even set foot on the rock yet, and views through binoculars can be notoriously deceptive, particularly head on. There couldn't be much up there to change our minds, but we owed it to ourselves to take one more look. Enough oxygen remained for that. If we were to write it off, at least we'd like to go as high as we could, just for the hell of it. So we left it up to the weather. In my diary I willed myself a little higher. "Tomorrow, if possible, I *will* get to the Couloir."

The twelfth started clear. I had the ice melting at six, and by eight, as the interior rain began to fall, we were through breakfasting on meat loaf from the evening before. Still, it was ten before we were under way. Half an hour later, even on a full flow of oxygen, Dave decided he couldn't make it. He had fared poorly, plagued with the same symptoms of incomplete acclimatization he'd had at Camp 1. This led to a lack of enthusiasm for the route, which made him possibly the only realist among us. We watched him safely back over the bergschrund to the tent, then reroped, with Barrel in the middle, and continued on to the Shoulder. Everest stood clear, rid even of its wind-blown banner. Ten thousand feet below the Rongbuk Glacier wound northward into brown Tibetan hills. Ice towers on the glacier appeared as hundreds of tiny, ice blue gems. Through binoculars we sighted the remains of the Rongbuk Monastery in the rubble left by the receding ice. It had been destroyed by the Chinese a few years before.

Yesterday's high point came easily by 1 P.M., then we were on new terrain. Clouds coalesced, a light snow fell, crampons scraped across outsloping rock and scratched superficially on glare ice. As I strolled along in the rear for the time, I mused on the inadequacies of an ice-ax arrest on such an ice-rink surface. Just don't fall, that's all, I thought. Climbing on his front crampon points, Willi led up a tiny fissure diagonally

transecting a bulge of glare ice. At the top he rammed his ax into the crack to belay Barrel. Waiting below, I discovered Barrel was tied in closer to me than to Willi. He would be unable to reach Willi's stance unless I moved along with him. His expression of astonishment as he turned to belay me and found me standing behind him was worth the lack of protection it cost in climbing up there.

With time for thoughts as we strolled along, I began to play games with my oxygen. Willi was leading on two liters. At that flow I could hold the pace with a reserve that allowed for reverie; on one liter it was an effort, and with the oxygen turned off I could barely keep up, my heart and lungs pounding to their limit. In another game, I would squeeze the entire contents of the rubber oxygen bladder into my lungs with a single, deep breath. In effect, this suddenly returned me to sea level. Within three or four seconds the bolus of well-oxygenated blood reached receptors, which sent their message to my brain. Momentarily my breathing almost ceased, and the fleeting respite from panting was pure pleasure. As the oxygen-rich blood reached my fingertips, they changed from purple to bright pink—and to purple again as I was suddenly returned to high altitude.

Perhaps there was too much time for thought. Somewhere during the course of our journey my objectivity succumbed to emotion. I decided the West Ridge was worth a try; I only hoped Willi would agree. Otherwise, we'd go clear to the base of the Couloir, if necessary, to convince him. Although this would mean wandering back to camp in the dark, the prospect seemed less forbidding at the moment than it should have.

At four we reached the rock, 25,100 feet, according to the altimeter. The Diagonal Ditch rose immediately above, to dissolve in fog and swirling snow. What we could see didn't look unreasonable, but we couldn't see much. We sat on the downsloping slabs, munching rum fudge.

"All right, Willi. Have you made up your mind? Or do we have to go higher still?"

"I'm convinced, Tom. This is far enough for today."

So the decision was made in the pit of our stomachs. Perhaps the day's walk had provided only the solitude for a necessary bit of introspection.

All doubts that might have lingered were removed moments later when we traversed the hundred yards to the ridge crest, where the West Shoulder butts against the mountain itself. Here, at the very inception of the West Ridge, was a flat platform of wind-rippled snow, roomy enough to house all the tents we would require. The far edge was bounded by a rock promontory from which we peered past our feet at the tiny cluster of tents nestled in the Western Cwm. The summit of Nuptse was directly across the way, now scarcely above us. Lhotse filled the end of the Cwm, for the first time unforeshortened. In the foreground Everest's South Face rose four thousand feet and fell an equal distance to the Cwm. The summit of the mountain was hidden. To the north, the slope rounded from view—dropping to the Rongbuk Glacier. The scene was clothed in a seductive beauty of boiling clouds, glazed golden by the brilliance of the evening sun, cloud shadows alternating with shafts of sunlight which bathed the ridges and reflected intensified from millions of tiny ice crystals floating in the cooling air. Was this the mountain's design to capture us? All doubt about our decision vanished with the spectacular dissolution of the storm. We headed down.

Dave was perplexed by our decision. He had been busy discarding food during our absence, convinced our departure the next day would be permanent.

"How did the route look?" he asked.

"Well, we really couldn't see much. Mighty cruddy rock though. But you should see the beautiful place for 4W. It's worth a try just to be able to live there a while."

And so the decision was made. We'd be back up. My diary reflected my weary bliss: "Tomorrow, if possible, I will go restfully to 2."

10. The Lost Weekend

WE REACHED the intersection with the main thoroughfare leading from Advance Base to the foot of the Lhotse face. It was now a well-worn groove in the snow. Slogging that last level quarter mile into camp, I consciously put a little more spring in my weary steps and noted Willi doing the same thing. The warm congratulations we received made us glow with satisfaction. "Great job," Big Jim shouted as Norm pumped our hands, and Will Siri smiled his agreement. "You reached 25,000 feet? How does it look above?" Chotari unfastened our crampons. Cups of steaming lemonade were thrust into our hands. The moment was ours.

But not for long. As we sat on food box seats around the food box table finishing lunch, Norman called a meeting. In our absence the South Colers had decided on four-man assault teams, instead of two-man teams, for the Col route. The first team would be Lute, Pownall, Big Jim, and Gombu. It hadn't been decided who would form the second team. Recalculating our original logistics they had concluded that four-man teams would require little more equipment and carries than called for in our original two-man estimates. Unprepared, and too weary to question, we accepted this with blind faith. Within a week or ten days, we were told, the South Col would be stocked for the final push. This would require that all the carrying power be thrown into the Col build-up for the present. The West Ridge would have to wait until they were through.

Only an American expedition would attempt to vote itself to the top of Everest. Our approach to decision making was at times exorbitantly democratic. The minority group, particularly if absent when the vote was taken, was inclined to suffer. We found ourselves preserved of the basic freedoms of speech, and the right to the pursuit of happiness (the West Ridge), but no inalienable rights to Sherpas. We were at a standstill. Norm offered us the opportunity of becoming the second team of four on the Col route. In the thin-walled privacy of our tent Willi and I mulled over events. His unconvincing rationalizations were an attempt to sooth my anger. I felt let down on something that I thought had been agreed upon by the entire expedition weeks before: that we should push the two routes simultaneously.

"Dammit, how could they do it to us? And four-man teams instead of two! That could ruin us, Willi. And it doesn't help their chances either! How can you be so damn calm?"

"Got to, Tom. Just to keep you out of trouble."

Two other events compounded the irony of the afternoon, making our commitment to the West Ridge irrevocable. Dave informed us he'd like to change to the Col route. The risks of the West Ridge seemed unjustifiable to him. "It's just not my kind of climbing." Jake's death had dealt the first blow to his enthusiasm, poor acclimatization the second. Later he told Willi that he feared my fanaticism would overextend the whole effort.

Barrel came into the tent that evening, glum and apologetic.

The mail, he said, bore grim news from the *National Geographic*. "I sure feel bad letting you fellows down, but I'm going to have to switch routes. I'd far rather tackle the West Ridge, but I'm on assignment and I am supposed to get pictures from the top. I've talked to Norm and he says I can go in the second assault. But, believe me, if it weren't for the pictures I'd be with you. And as soon as we get done I'll be back over and do everything I can in support."

"Sure, Barrel," Willi replied, "we understand. It's tough. I don't envy you, having to climb Everest by the Col."

What had once been a team of seven was now three and a half: Barry, Willi, me, and, as a question mark because of his health, Dick. How could we possibly hope to climb a new route on the highest mountain in the world with so few Sahibs? And no Sherpas? Maybe we should take Norm up on his offer, and flush the West Ridge? Nuts. That's no way to climb a mountain. The Col route's been paved. All we have to do is stroll up in their footsteps.

"No," I said to Willi, "let's talk them out of a couple of Sherpas and try to make the winch work. There's no other possibility."

We were stripped to the bone of manpower, but we were a core of like-thinking individuals. We would rather try the unknown and fail than risk being successful on what Tashi had dubbed "the old milk run," though who had added this expression to his colorful vocabulary I could only guess. That evening we declined Norm's offer, presented our plan to try the winch, and won Tashi and Nima Tenzing to help us in the days ahead. The first threat to our existence was past, and though we were hardly running, at least we were still alive. My entry into Emerson's diary for that night was "Tomorrow, if possible, *I will* calculate logistics for the West Ridge."

To Gene I wrote: "This brings me to some of the imponderables. Why do the four of us isolate ourselves from the optimal chance to stand on the highest point of this earth? Something about the Col route, not to sell it short, is too familiar, too traveled. Not that I wouldn't go to the summit by it if the West Ridge failed; I would. But do not be surprised or disappointed to find your husband's name among the missing when the clippings pour forth. Also do not feel I will be missing fulfillment, for whether or not I find it on the West Ridge, I know it does not lie in wait as the 9th, 10th, 11th, or 12th, or even the 1st American to climb Mount Everest by the South Col.

"More positively, there's the real attraction of a new route, a route that looks feasible for a small determined group. The challenge is to see if we can pull it off on a shoestring—with an adequate margin of safety but without unlimited reserves. Our hope is lightness, speed, and a hell of a lot of luck. Still I marvel at the relative ease with which I decided to bypass a much greater guarantee of success for a bit more challenge and gamble, a bit more opportunity for failure—and therefore a lot more feeling of accomplishment should we pull it off."

It was what Willi called, "the spiritual, moral, and mountaineering correctness of the only route worthy of our efforts."

* * *

One day bled into another; our progress was limited to replotting logistics, paring a little food here, eliminating oxygen or a tent there. Before we were through we had reduced the size of our effort to almost half our earlier estimate.

About 8 A.M., timed perfectly with the sun, Danu would make his rounds and outside our tent we would hear, "Good morning, Sahib. Tea?" It came sometimes with sugar, sometimes with milk and sugar; after a time I developed a growing lack of interest in tea of any form, and it became merely a medicine to help maintain hydration. There were days when I would open half an eye, mumble a drugged "No thanks," and retreat deeper into my cocoon for an extra hour's sleep before breakfast. Other times I would clutch the warm cup in both hands, sipping so slowly that the tea was only half gone when Mingma came to pick up the cups. Willi downed his quickly and dove back into *The Making of a President, 1960,* reading aloud to his lazy companion.

Looking over at me one morning he asked, "What time did you get to sleep last night?"

"Couple of hours ago, I guess. But boy what a lot of thoughts I had. I replotted the logistics for the last two camps. All we need above Camp 4 are one two-man Gerry tent and one four-man Drawtite."

"How do you figure that?"

"Well, its sort of like musical tents. The recon team will take the Gerry over for their night at 5W. When the first assault comes the next day the four Sherpas will bring a big Drawtite to sleep in while the climbers use the Gerry. Then we'll just unpitch the Gerry and take it up to 6W on the final carry."

Finally, comprehending the genius behind this maneuver, Willi said, "The only hooker is if the recon team gets down too late to get back to 4W the same day, it'll be a mite crowded with four men sitting up all night in a two-man tent."

"Well, that adds a bit of sport," I said. "Do you think we can get by on only one flashlight for each summit team? And one radio each?"

"Sure. But we'll have to carry the radios over the top. They're too good to leave behind."

And so it went. The daylight hours were often spent doing little and accomplishing less in our high sunny world, trapped between the walls of Nuptse and Everest. The heat and stillness were oppressive. Sometimes I would want to take my temperature to make sure I wasn't sick, but it was only glacier lassitude —we called it the "Cwm gloom," which was not gloom but a delightful lethargy that must be the Himalayan substitute for sex. We would postpone from one day to the next the releveling of our tent site to avoid sleeping—or not sleeping—in a corkscrew, downhill position. Each afternoon clouds filled the Khumbu Valley, then spilled over into the Cwm. The enervating heat gave way to light snowfall and a delightful coolness as the cloud engulfed us.

"Let's bring in Lester and brainwash him," I suggested to Willi one day.

"Good idea. Every psychologist must have problems."

We would spend the afternoons flat on our backs in the tent, analyzing each other.

"Well, there's not much use trying to make Hornbein over," Willi said, "he's so satisfied with his miserable existence the way it is now."

Others were not in the sack so much of the time. Lute Jerstad and Dick Pownall reached the South Col on April 16, an incredibly early date compared to past expeditions. They came into Advance Base dead tired but triumphant at 9:30 that night with souvenirs from the junkyard at the Col.

"You mean you actually had your mittens off up there? Wasn't it windy?"

"Yes," said Pownall, "but it wasn't too cold. The Sherpas kept right up without oxygen. Chotari knew a shortcut around the Geneva Spur but we didn't discover it till after we'd gone over the top."

"By the way, Tom," said Lute, "my oxygen lasted nine hours on a three-liter flow."

That was fine, but there wasn't that much oxygen in a bottle. It was time for me to recalibrate the regulators.

We were at an altitude above which man cannot stay indefinitely. The highest permanent habitation is at about 17,500 feet in Bolivia. One cannot stay healthy much higher. For permanent mountain populations, survival is difficult; the miscarriage rate is too high—but then that wasn't a problem for us. Nevertheless, at 21,350 feet our Advance Base Camp was above the mysterious line, and we were all keyed to detect the first signs of high-altitude deterioration: little, nonspecific things, such as increased irritability, loss of appetite, weakness, and waning enthusiasm for the task at hand. At dinner, plates would be left half full. Even Barry Prather, who had consumed more than 8,000 calories a day lower down, just nibbled at his food. Dick Pownall's once massive legs wasted as he sat and stared at, and considered tasteless, the repast set before him. Complaints increased as our diet became more boring.

"We're having chicken tetrazzini again tonight? We had it last night."

"No, that was chicken á-la-king. Can't you tell the difference?"

"No, it all tastes like cardboard."

The periodic weighing sessions that were part of Will's research demoralized us further.

"I've lost thirty pounds already."

"That's nothing. I'm down thirty-eight." Will seemed invariably to select a cold, windy day, ask us to strip to our string underwear, then complain when he couldn't read the oscillations on the dial of his bathroom scale because we were shivering so hard. "Just take the extremes and average them, Will," I suggested.

Dick Emerson deteriorated best. On the approach march his thighs had split the seams of his walking shorts; now he was fighting his own battle. It began before we reached Base Camp. Each time he went up to 21,000 feet his draining sinuses and parched throat would force him into a bout of coughing soon after each meal. This triggered a hyperactive gag reflex. Dick would sit at the table, nibbling willfully at his food, command-

ing each bite to please stay down. Soon he would rise, walk quietly out of the tent, and shortly return to start over again without a word, perhaps by sipping some tea. One evening there was fruit cocktail for dessert. Dick looked at it and the old twinkle returned to his eyes. That ought to stay down, he thought, and as we all watched anxiously he slowly ate his own and several other servings donated to the cause. Then the twinkle faded, and he rose and left the tent again. His strength declined with his weight and he soon had to go down to Base to fatten up for the next high siege, hoping it would be with the mountain and not his stomach.

Willi and I attacked the problem of eating with a stubborn determination born of our Masherbrum experience. There I lost twenty pounds, which didn't leave much. We knew on Everest that with time our menu would grow old, so we stuffed ourselves. As long as there was food, we ate. We would neatly clean the leftovers of those whose appetites were jading, and we competed even in this. In due course we would stagger distended to our tents to sit dazed and breathless on our sleeping bags, barely able to bend over and untie our boots. For all our discomfort, however, we lost only four pounds each during the weeks preceding our final push. We explained this glibly to our companions as merely the superior acclimatization of our hardened Himalayan digestive tracts. Our doctors, Gil and Dave, suspected that no matter how much one consumed, little would be utilized. Whatever our inner mysteries, Willi and I believed that our devouring determination helped to slow the process of deterioration.

One event that invariably followed our distensive eating was the cool hour, which easily became the "cruel hour"—the few fleeting minutes each evening when we rose from our orgy, left the warmth of the mess tent, and hurried off to bed through the cold gray evening light of the Cwm. It was then that the *Why?* knifed me, and thoughts of home and the warm beach at La Jolla mocked us in our icy isolation half a world away. We would stand before the sleeve entrance to our small tent, summon courage, bend down, and plunge inside. On hands and knees I poked my head through the sleeve, kicked boots together outside to dislodge the snow from the cleats. Inside, panting from the labor, we lit our candle lanterns to enjoy their psychological warmth. We shed our down parkas, wadding them for pillows or stuffing them between our sleeping bags and air mattresses to insulate our shoulders and hips against the cold emanating from the snow below. We tucked our boots under our air mattresses to fill concavities the heat from our bodies melted in the snow beneath us. Then we slid into cold sleeping bags. We would shiver a while, and the cruel hour was over.

Wrapped in womblike warmth, lit by the glow of our lanterns, we would lie back and accept the security and comfort of the moment. Our world was now complete within the compass of cloth walls. In a duffel at our feet were all the earthly possessions that mattered: down pants, extra goggles, socks, cleaner underwear saved for the final assault, our luxuries in the corner by our heads—candles, pills to loosen a cough or to dry a sinus or to lull a sleepless thinker, diaries and stationery, toothbrush, mirror, lotion, pictures of the people we loved, and a copy of that 1954 *Mountain World* that contained our only photo of the West Ridge. A drawstring bolted out the cold snowy world and there was more than comfort within.

But there were chores for those who clung to a few of the amenities. Willi, deeply engrossed in the complexities of Emerson's diary, would steel himself against the aural ordeal of my toothbrushing. Propped on an elbow, I would engineer a bit of toothpowder (paste freezes) onto my brush. Then would come the sounds of vigorous massage accompanied by exclamations about the joys of oral hygiene, all prelude to a loud gulp—the only convenient means of disposal. Besides it helped maintain precious body fluids. The final toothbrush-cleaning slurp was anticlimatic. The ordeal was over, and Willi could settle back to his labors. He never brushed his teeth.

The diary was part of Dick's research into motivation and our response to everything from weather to each others' annoyances. Each book was indestructibly constructed and emblazoned with our names in gold; no matter which crevasse we might try to leave one in, a smiling Sherpa face would always appear: "You lose book, Sahib?" We were asked to pour forth our most evil thoughts and fondest hopes in an impersonalized numerical scale a computer could ultimately sink its transistors into. Our emotions were all to lie within a range of minus 5 to plus 5. We had to appraise weather past and future, rate each other's irritability, evaluate the climbing difficulties and dangers today and tomorrow, gauge our physical condition (weak-strong), our enthusiasm for the various routes, and estimate the chance of success. There was room for a "Decision made in the last 8 days." True to my profession I wrote: "(1) To wait for sinusitis to resolve. (2) To take cold pills. (3) To take antibiotic. (4) To take both cold pill and antibiotics. Outcome 3."

Chores done, we could turn to pocketbooks, or letters to wives, or talk.

"I'm afraid I violated the law today," I told Willi. "Lester was sitting outside his tent, tanning his Freudian hide, and I happened to glance down at some papers he left out. The one on top was one Emerson had filled out, where you're asked to rate how you think others feel toward you. He's underestimating our regard for him. All he put down was an 80."

"He must be really feeling guilty," Willi said. "All he's done is come up here, vomit, and head back to Base again. He must feel bad that he hasn't been able to help on the route. But gosh, he just doesn't know how we feel."

"He's got more determination than anybody on the team and it's all used up trying to make his food stay down. I hope he doesn't come up too soon this time. Maybe if he stays till the final push, he can get up and over before he has time to start vomiting again."

Dick's recurrent loss of fluid through vomiting could only aggravate the dehydration that is always a problem in high-altitude mountaineering. A man breathing fast and deep into cold dry air may lose a gallon of water a day. It is so hard to prime and light stoves to melt large volumes of snow to small volumes of water that great drinking orgies don't take place. Dehydration is an important cause of deterioration above 21,000 feet. Knowing this and having portable butane stoves which would light instantly, we went to the other extreme. Moreover we had the luxury of a Sherpa cook at Advance Base. So we would down tea, soup, coffee, and Wyler's lemonade by the quart, often far exceeding the loss we could expect from a normal day's work.

For some reason, the effects of all this liquid never pressed upon us during the day when there was unlimited voiding acreage available. However, as soon as we lay down at night, our kidneys turned on. But this was a $400,000 expedition, so we did not have to emerge from our cozy shelter into the cold world. Each of us had a sleek plastic Italian-designed urinal, personalized, which we carried faithfully wherever we went. One need not even leave his sleeping bag, or, with a bit of practice, even leave a horizontal position to use the thing. Some mastered the technique sooner than others. A few never quite got the hang of it. Still I had to give Willi credit for trying.

Willi could put down his book, blow out his candle, and within minutes vigorously concoct dreams to regale Lester with next morning. I would plod through *Justine* until my candle burned out, then continue in my sleeping bag with flashlight, waiting for sleep. Finally, tired of reading, I often lay wake until early morning, climbing the Ridge a hundred times, imagining the difficulties of the first step, the problems of rope fixing and piton pounding on an overhang at 28,000 feet, climbing without oxygen because the difficulty was too great to allow the extra weight. My brain pored over prosaic logistics: the numbers of food boxes, oxygen bottles, carries from 4W to 5W, Sherpas we could borrow from the Colers. I was obsessed with the mountain and escaped only when I could dream of Gene and our children, finally to sleep through the hours of dawn and morning tea.

My obsession worried Dick. "You'd better slow down," he said to me one morning at Advance Base. "Your enthusiasm is so outspoken you may be threatening Willi's role as climbing leader. I think he might resent it a bit."

"I can't believe it. Do you really think so?"

"Well, yes. For example, the radio conversations. That's part of Willi's job, talking to Norm and the others. You should stay out of it."

"I'd never thought of it before, but I think you're right. It's my tunnel vision showing through. Even so, it's hard to believe he could be jealous or resentful. He's never said a thing."

"Well, think about it and keep your eyes open."

Sitting alone in the tent, I had a chance to think. In my zeal for the climb I had become so absorbed in the problems of planning and fighting for the West Ridge that I never dreamed I might be pressing Willi. He was our climbing leader. Should we ever not agree, then the decision would be his. He had an understanding and insight that I envied. He could talk with Norm and the others at times when my outspoken responses irked them. Yet the thought of not being natural, of now being at all servile, seemed quite wrong. In my usual, subtle manner, I could find no solution but to just point-blank ask him how he felt.

That night, filling out my diary, I reached the blank for "Decisions made in the last 8 days." All right. *Now.*

"Willi, do you resent my talking on the radio when it's supposed to be your job as climbing leader?"

"What? Where did you get that idea?"

"Well, Dick thought I might be stepping on your toes as leader. He thought you might resent it. Do you?"

"Well, son, as long as you remember who's the leader of this affair, go ahead and talk on the radio all you want."

"No, seriously, you baboon, how do you feel?"

"Well, I'll tell you. As they said, you're a fanatic. With you around, I don't figure I have to worry about all the things my old guide's instinct has had me doing for years. Even when I'm asleep, I can hear you lying awake over there at night, with the gears grinding out new ideas. I figure all I've got to do is wake up in the morning to the deluge, filter out what sounds good, and keep you from starting a civil war with the Colers. And just keep the old Unsoeld talents ready when you finally crack.

"I don't know whether to say thanks or not. Anyway, I'm relieved. But don't hold your breath till I crack. At your age, you'll never make it."

The conversation degenerated. I decided not to talk on the radio again when Willi was available. Instead I devoted our evening hours to brainwashing him. Only when it looked as if our effort was threatened by expedition politics did I ever forget my vow.

It soon became apparent to me that the Colers had miscalculated how much equipment the four-man summit teams would need. Instead of a week or ten days to stock the South Col, it would be closer to twice that. Even with luck the earliest they could reach the summit was the end of April.

Hope for the survival of our West Ridge effort thus depended, in the absence of Sherpas, on an untried system; the battle of the winch was begun of necessity. But would the engine run at these altitudes? Could we find suitable terrain —long snow slopes free from crevasses and cliffs in the fall line, and having adequate terminals? The route to the Shoulder did not fit the description. It climbed up-Cwm over scree and icefall, then descended a couple of hundred feet past the Old Dump, turned a steep corner to the New Dump, and finally climbed steeply to the skyline crest below Camp 3W. Only here did the prospect for hauling seem hopeful. Our supplies would be lashed to a sled formed from three pairs of short skis held together at each end by a metal crossbar. A thin steel line led to the tiny winch, anchored out of sight above. With an exotic mixture of rocket fuels blended especially for the altitude, the 16-pound engine was supposed to drag 500 pounds uphill at 5 feet per minute. In our naïve anticipation the rig seemed simple, but we soon saw that our team sorely lacked rapport with it. The day Barry Prather came up from Base, we thought we had our solution, a man who could make a motor run. Unfortunately, the South Colers got him first. He joined Dingman to make the Lhotse Summit team—while we wondered what had happened to the plan that the West Ridge would come second only to the Col.

Al Auten came to our rescue. As communications officer, he had seemed indispensably wed to the short-wave radio at Base; however, when we asked Norman if Noddy or Maynard Miller could be trained to take over the radio, Al was agreeable. Forlorn though our effort might be, he was glad to escape the nightly exchange with Kathmandu for a chance to climb. We became a team of five, and he and Barry headed up to the Shoul-

der to establish a winch station below 3 W and string cable down to the New Dump.

The next day, in a blizzard, they huddled over the motor trying to make it start. Fine snow filled the carburetor and diluted the fuel. The starter broke. When they retreated to the tent to attempt repairs and had the housing off, the starter spring suddenly uncoiled across the tent. They stuffed it back in. The engine would occasionally gasp, sputter, or sigh, and a quantity of nuts, bolts, and springs had no place to go when it came time to reassemble things.

So on April 19 Willi and I headed up with a new motor. Willi carried his trusty old Kelty pack frame, and I experimented with a new fiberglass wrap-around model. Encased by the pack and an excess of down clothing, I felt secure against the cold, but before we had traveled two hundred yards I was bathed in sweat from ankles to neck, while my toes, nose, fingers, and forehead felt leadenly frozen. Wind blasted my face and accentuated the contrast. With each step I fought to expand my lungs within my rigid shell. When Willi paused, I complained of his grueling pace, then collapsed panting, freezing, and sweating in various parts, as he delivered the final taunt:

"You better head down to Base for some rest tomorrow. You're not quite up to keeping up with the Old Man yet."

If I can just make it to the Old Dump, I told myself. Willi plowed ahead, the rope taut between us. Maybe he's right, I thought; maybe I do need to go down. When it looked most as if I would never get there, Willi made his mistake.

"Let me take your pack; you can take my Kelty."

"No," I said, "yours is just as heavy. It won't do any good. It's just not my day."

"Well, let me try carrying that monster anyway. I'm curious."

We traded and I took the lead. My torso began to cool, my nose to warm, and my breathing to be easier, now that I was free of the Iron Maiden. The rope came taut behind as I pushed to the edge of exhaustion, hoping I wasn't holding us up too much. Up the fixed rope we went, not pausing, over the crest, down to the tents at the Dump.

"Where in the world were you going in such a rush?" Willi asked.

"I was just trying to keep you off my heels. Wasn't that why you put me in the lead?"

"Well, you taxed the Old Guide a bit. Just goes to show you the virtues of a good pack."

Barry and Al met us at the *New* New Dump for lunch. Though discouraged, they were determined to make the damned winch go. They headed back up with their new supplies. Four days later they came down, the machine still master. Willi and Dick took the next shift, then Barry replaced Willi. The hand winch was installed at the New New Dump, cable was strung diagonally down the slope, and the sled piled high with oxygen bottles. Cranking began: thirty seconds, forty-five, and that was all we could do. Even Tashi and Nima Tenzing couldn't crank much longer. Slowly the stretch came out of the cable, then the sled broke loose and inched up. A foot, two feet, three, and stop. More cranking, more stretch, and up it jerked again.

Dick used his ice ax as a snatch block to change the direction of the cable so as to keep the sled from drifting across the slope toward a large crevasse. The ax broke loose, soaring across the face to impale itself in the snow a hundred feet away. As Dick watched helplessly, the sled rolled sideways, penduluming across the slope into the crevasse. Out of sight above, Barry and the two Sherpas kept cranking, unaware that the sled, with its treasure of oxygen bottles, spun slowly in space. Slowly the sled rose to the lip of the crevasse, arced over the edge, and disappeared above.

Once both sleds reached the New New Dump, hand winching ended. With Nima Tenzing sick, the effort became impossible. Another round with the motor was only briefly successful. One sled now hung five hundred feet below the ridge crest, visible from Advance Base as a black speck. Finally, the afternoon snows buried it, and it took more than a day to find it again. The idea of our having misplaced three hundred pounds of oxygen bottles seemed ridiculous to those of us watching from below. Mechanical inaptitude and a growing antiwinch bias prevented my helping. I could imagine an oxygen-laden sled plunging spectacularly Cwmward, our hopes for the West Ridge riding with it. With each near disaster, my conservatism deepened. We had better not tempt Everest's gods. It would be so much safer to go the old-fashioned way and carry the loads.

The day finally came when the motor, guided by the steely hand of Auten, was made to run and finish the hauling. In the end we may have saved a day or two and at the least the winch provided good group therapy. In the words of Barry Corbet: "Never has so little been accomplished by so many."

A little manpower would obviously be better. Accordingly, at Advance Base I was always on the prowl for any loose Sherpas to ferry loads to our Dump. An occasional sick cast-off from the Col, and Mingma, our eager untalented cook, could be coerced into carrying a couple of food boxes the two-hour journey up. Slowly, we acquired Sherpas, sometimes having as many as three or four. On April 25, unescorted Sherpas were turned around on the Col route by the weather. This was a crucial carry, the most demanding of the entire route; thirty-eight loads in all had to be carried from 25,000 feet to the Col without use of oxygen.

The morning of April 26 a steady snowfall added to the South Colers' depression from the failure of the day before. We had been at 21,000 feet for almost a month. Four days earlier, Willi had proposed that some of us should descend to Base for rest and to slow down the drain on high-camp food, which seemed to disappear as fast as it arrived, leaving too little to stock the higher camps. The idea was vetoed, since deterioration was not evident and everyone claimed he was feeling fine. But on the 26th, growing impatient to be on with it, and realizing that we couldn't stay so high and healthy indefinitely, we held another critical meeting:

"If I had known some members of this expedition were going to be so fanatical about the West Ridge . . ." Norman began. He reminded us that the West Ridge had been his dream too, long ago. But now a carry had failed and time had been lost; our strength was supposedly declining with the long stay up high.

"There's no question we're deteriorating," Will Siri said. "One more day just sitting and we may be too far gone for the final push. Remember, it's five more days from here to the summit, living higher every day. Tomorrow, we either have to start the final assault or all go down to recuperate."

"But, Will," I piped up, "four days ago you said there was no sign of deterioration. How can it have suddenly progressed so far that one more day makes such a big difference?"

"Be quiet, Tom," Willi said. And I was, feeling certain he would rise articulately to the occasion, for we both knew what was coming. Twenty-one loads still had to be carried to the Col. If the assault were to begin tomorrow, this would require all the Sherpas available. The West Ridge would have to wait.

Norm made the final decision: "If the weather's good tomorrow, we'll start the final push. If not, we'll go down to rest."

The meeting was over, we were overruled, and Willi hadn't said a thing. But what was there to say?

We rehashed the meeting with Dick, who had come up to Advance Base that afternoon for the third time, arriving two hours too late to join the battle. Though the West Ridge was at a standstill, the setback didn't seem too serious considering the time remaining. We did have an obligation to climb the mountain and the Col route offered the best chance of success. I could understand the South Colers' feelings. Inactivity had led to impatience, a brief storm to pessimism, and the loss of time to fear of failure. Still, we had a full month's lead on any previous expedition, so the decision seemed downright premature. I could understand, but I couldn't agree. The thing that bit deepest was the realization that, outside our nucleus of five, there seemed to be no enthusiasm for the West Ridge. Our dream was now to be disregarded; views expressed and decisions made in the detachment of the approach march were now being modified, and I could see no reason why. What puzzled me most was Willi's silence. Why hadn't he spoken up? Usually we complemented each other, I outspoken in defense of the Ridge, he tactfully pacifying, though no less motivated. If he sometimes felt my responses were too extreme, I now thought his far too passive. Perhaps we drove each other deeper into our own patterns in an effort to compensate for the deficit each thought he saw in the other.

April 27 was immaculately clear, the sky blue-black, and the plume for once missing from Everest. Shortly after lunch, Big Jim, Norman, Gombu, and Ang Dawa set out with thirteen Sherpas. I felt the excitement of the moment. The end of their journey lay eight thousand feet above and only five days away if the weather held. I felt envy, pride, admiration, and hope that they would pull it off. There was something missing when they left.

A day later Lute, Barrel, Dick Pownall, and Girme Dorje headed up. I ran the movie camera to immortalize their departure. The next day, I took Barry to trade off with Willi on the winch. Even with a load we made excellent time. Willi, too, was effusive in describing his feat of step-cutting across the fixed ropes—with sixty-five pounds on his back. For us, at least, acclimatization was still a jump ahead of deterioration. With Dave, Barry Prather, and the last Sherpas headed toward the Col, Advance Base was a ghost town that night, and we were no closer to our destination than we had been weeks before.

On the 30th, as the final assault team moved up to their final camp, Willi and I headed toward Base for some unneeded recuperation. Going down was a journey of little pleasure and of mixed emotions. We had been relentlessly pushing for weeks, both on the mountain and in the battles to keep the effort alive. Now, on the day before the final assault by the Col, we found ourselves headed in the opposite direction, carrying us farther from our goal. It reminded me of a Monopoly game, where you suddenly land on a square that says, "Go back to go" and you start over. We walked into base that afternoon. The summit of Everest towered eleven thousand feet above our heads, just as it had when we first arrived six weeks before.

. . . Naked of life, naked of warmth and safety, bare to the sun and stars, beautiful in its stark snowy loneliness, the Mountain waits. . . .

Those who will attack it, must stand ready for that meeting to strip themselves of all the ordinary things that men desire, all the normal; and easy and gracious things of life—ready even, if need be, to give up life, itself. In return, the Mountain offers them hardship, and danger, . . . and an unattainable goal.—It tests them with stern trials. Such a peak seldom need exert its strength. For the little insects who challenge its immensities, it sets high the conditions of victory; and it lets them defeat themselves. Every secret weakness of body or mind or spirit will be mercilessly bared Only if some persist, if, stripped to essentials, they continue the fight, then at last it will act. And it is far stronger than they. There is no shame in being beaten by such an antagonist. . . .

But to those men who are born for mountains, the struggle can never end, until their lives end. To them, it holds the very quintessence of living—the fiery core, after the lesser parts have been burned away. . . .

On earth there is nothing physically greater than the great unconquered peaks. There is nothing more beautiful. Among their barren snows they hide the ultimate simplicity of spiritual splendor. . . .

—Elizabeth Knowlton

11. Our Turn

MAY 1. Fresh eggs, chicken, even a can of beer that had somehow escaped prior consumption, then a bucket of warm water for a piecemeal bath in the morning sunshine, followed by clean underwear and socks after a month —it all took a bit of the edge off our regrets at coming down. It was a relief for me—and for Willi too, I suspect—to escape for a few days from my nervous energy.

The morning was warm and sunny, but streamers of snow blew like prayer flags off the crest of Nuptse, carrying far out across the Cwm. Could they even move under such conditions? The whole battle seemed remote, unreal, unimportant. Here in the shelter of towering peaks, where weeks before all had been frozen, water coursed in rivulets over the surface of the Glacier. Base Camp looked well worn and lived in. The red tents seemed a permanent part of the moraine. Paths had been cleared and lined with rocks. A stone-sided, tarp-roofed kitchen had been constructed; inside, box shelves were half-filled with long-forgotten delicacies too heavy to be carried farther up the mountain. There were chairs to lounge in and a slightly sagging table to write on and eat from. There was no use fighting it.

We busied ourselves with chores. I sharpened my ax, made new bindings for my crampons, read *From Russia with Love*. We weighed in on Siri's scale; at 131 pounds I was only four below normal, even with the dirt washed off. Willi had lost about the same. Perhaps our eating habits were paying off.

From Camp 4 on the Lhotse Face, Dingman reported high winds and no sign of movement above. Prather, he informed us, had had breathing trouble during the night, possibly pulmonary edema. Dave had given him digitalis and some oxygen the Sherpas had uncovered outside the tent. He was better today, but weak.

At 3 P.M. on May 2, the eight Sherpas who had carried the high camp reached Base. They were tired. "Camp 6 very high, Sahib," Nawang Dorje reported proudly, but that would not matter if the wind had kept them pinned down all day. An hour later the radio squawked to life with Gil's voice from Advance Base.

Gil (Advance Base): The clouds have lifted up here and we see nine climbers descending from above the Yellow Band and an additional three between Camps 4 and 3. Don't yet know what all this means—whether they have been successful or are retreating.

Our conversation with Kathmandu at 5:00 that evening found Bill Gresham's radio shack packed in tense anticipation.

"No word," was all Al Auten could offer to Jim Ullman. But ten minutes after we signed off, the Base set came to life.

Roberts: 2 to Base. 2 to Base. Come in Base!

Auten: This is Base. Go ahead 2.

Roberts: Three people are down. The Big One and the Small One made the top! Over.

Auten: Hallelujah! What news!

Then, recovering his usual radio calm, Al said, "Sure. Whittaker and Gombu, we're assuming. Is that correct? Over."

Roberts: It is Roger, but not for release, not for release. Over.

They'd made it. In spite of the winds, they'd made it! Willi and I hugged each other with a feeling of relief. Relief—and pleasure, too—at their success. Jim and Gombu had given us our chance to try the West Ridge. But we couldn't completely share the elation of our companions. For us it was premature; we had scarcely begun. I wrote that evening, "I envy Whittaker only in having his effort behind him, while ours is solidly, challengingly before us."

Nawang Dorje came to ask for fuel for celebration. Will gave him a bottle of Scotch, which Nawang accepted with a mischievous grin. Though the Sherpas appeared less excited about the success than we, they weren't going to pass up an excuse for a party. Will and Maynard felt like celebrating too and Noddy joined them. After a while, Willi and I headed for bed. A tremendous weight had been lifted. As we lay in our bags, thinking of the future, we could hear Maynard talking in the mess tent, fifty feet away.

"Now that the mountain is climbed we've got to put our major effort into research," he said. Will's softer reply was lost in the night breeze. Willi and I were suddenly alert. We turned around on our air mattresses and slid our heads out the vestibule of the tent. The lantern on the table in the mess tent cast silhouettes of the tent's three occupants on its red-orange wall. We watched and listened attentively, picking up only tantalizing snatches of conversation.

Our effort was more wonderfully rewarded by the beauty of the night. It was alive with sound—the roar of remote wind off high ridges, water trickling in tiny rivulets over the surface of the glacier, the deep settling *whoompf* which said the glacier had moved. Moonlight touched the half-imagined walls of Nuptse, and reflected brilliantly from the many-facets of *névé penitentes* on the glacier below. My thoughts wandered upward from the crumbled chaos of the Khumbu Glacier, past the West Shoulder —home.

Days passed as Willi and I lazily fattened. The afternoon of May 5, we went to our tent, bored and impatient, and I to my diary:

"Weather was too poor for Norman to come from Advance Base yesterday, so we expect him down this P.M. Now we can have at the West Ridge in earnest, but with not much time remaining.

"To add to the excitement and to our difficulties, yesterday four Sherpas cooking tea in the tents at the Dump were suddenly accosted by a powder-snow avalanche. It carried them several hundred feet downhill, rolling them up in the tents, and providing a nice ride down. Their axes, crampons, and ropes, sitting outside, were lost. They came down to Advance Base without them, but able to laugh at the whole episode. Fortunately almost all our supplies were at the New Dump and hopefully are unscathed. All four kept their good humor as they descended to

Base Camp for rest, but only Passang Tendi volunteered to go up on the West Ridge again."

About midafternoon a buzz of excited voices brought us out of the tent. Several figures moved slowly toward Camp. In front Dingman traveled with weary resignation. Norman's Sherpa, Ang Dawa, still moved like a lithe spider monkey; but Norman came slowly, each slightly-wide-based step taken with the painful deliberation of a man almost drained dry. He appeared more than just tired; he had aged considerably.

Within an hour of his arrival we were all gathered at the table in the mess tent. There were things to be discussed and, with a strange urgency, Norm wanted to discuss them now. Should we release the names of the summit team? No, we had decided during the approach march to avoid or try to avoid making a hero of the first American in such a team effort; we'd wait until all attempts had been completed. But now, Will Siri pointed out, the Sherpas could not be held to this strange pact, and word would leak back to Kathmandu within a few days. Dingman agreed. Big Jim agreed too; he felt that all publicity would be good for the Expedition. The majority voted to wait.

Norm was impatient to move on. His lined, windblasted face showed fatigue. His eyes, set deep, seemed empty, as if he had gone some place and had not completely returned.

He began as he had ten days before at Advance Base: "If I had known Tom was going to be so fanatical about the West Ridge," he said, and this time he finished the thought, "I would have increased our budget, ordered three hundred oxygen bottles, and hired fifty Sherpas. If only Tom had been honest with me about his ambitions back in the States."

"I'm sorry, Norm, I guess I wasn't aware of my own ambitions back then," I replied, puzzled.

The Maytag oxygen mask worked wonderfully, he said, but the plastic sleeping masks were unbearable. The main mistake, he felt, was insufficient oxygen; not nearly enough had been allotted for two four-man ascents of Everest, plus Lhotse. By implication, too much had been assigned to the West Ridge. Willi, sitting beside me, placed a hand gently on my shoulder, anticipating a volatile rebuttal. I remained silent, waiting.

Norm described the extreme breathlessness of just sitting inside the tent at 27,000 feet. The oxygen left in his climbing bottle helped. When it was gone, anxiety and air hunger returned. Another bottle was started. Perhaps there was logic in its continued use considering what they would be called upon to do the following day. Regardless, Norm needed it; the others would benefit by it also. During their two nights at Camp 6 almost all the eighteen bottles carried there were consumed. Six had been meant for the second assault.

Basing our oxygen needs on the experience of the British and the Swiss Expeditions, I had not reckoned on a supply of "sitting" oxygen. If we used it only for climbing and sleeping, there was more than enough oxygen for all our objectives. Now, Norm raised the question: Was this adequate? He had been higher than most of us, and could speak with an authority that even the Masherbrum group didn't have. He needed more oxygen; the rest of us might too.

Norm, at 45, had climbed higher than any man his age. To film the summit climb he and Ang Dawa, burdened with cameras, had gone above 28,000 feet before their oxygen ran low. As he talked, I began to realize that he had traveled to the edge of physical limits—oxygen almost had led him beyond. He was exhausted, possibly disappointed, perhaps suffering the lingering effects of oxygen lack, and his restraint was gone. His feelings poured forth. There was nothing to say in reply, in my own defense; there was no need. I turned and looked at Willi's hand on my shoulder, then at Willi, and the hand relaxed.

A discussion of the future followed. For once the West Ridge was free of attack. Lute and Barry were eager for another chance, so it was decided they would wait at Base until the West Ridge team was in position, then move up, hopefully to reach the summit by the Col the same day we came up the West Ridge. Unfortunately, with ten men having gone as high as the South Col, about seventy-five of the ninety-five bottles of oxygen were consumed to get only two men to the top; just enough remained to permit one two-man assault by the Col, with a two-man support. It was our turn now; all we had to do was climb the mountain.

The next morning we sat in the sunshine sorting gear and chatting with Jimmy Roberts about our Sherpa requirements. Perhaps our lack of haste was a reluctance to surrender the security of Base Camp for the physical and emotional effort we knew waited above. Leaving an hour late, we headed for the sun-baked oven of the Icefall. Almost with the first steps onto the ice our mood changed to one of pleasure at moving our legs, climbing, panting, sweating, coming alive again. The pleasure was heightened by our feeling of pleasant finality at heading up for the last time. No matter what happened in the next two weeks, the effort would soon be over. Life could take on a new direction.

We dragged into Advance Base in time for supper. Al was there with Dick and Barry, who had descended in forlorn frustration from another round with the winch. After supper we had problems to solve.

"Where are you going to house the Sherpas?" Barry asked.

"At the Dump," Willi replied.

"You're kidding," Dick said.

"No, why should I be kidding? That was just a surface slide that swept the camp away."

"It's nothing to gamble with," said Gil.

Dick agreed. "It was a continuous small surface slide that could have killed them."

"It's only a veneer about five inches thick," I said. "That's all that's going to come off that slope any time, Dick."

"Now, just a minute Tom; a very small percentage of the slope that could come did come. What kept the rest of it up there I don't know, but the very small section that did come completely buried the tent. It didn't just roll over it, it consumed it."

"How far down the hill is the tent?" I asked.

"I'm not sure," Dick answered. "The one that was buried, I don't think ever moved. Those guys were very unlucky to get hit with a slide, but given that they were going to get hit they were just damnably lucky, just extremely lucky."

"But this is always the case, Dick; you're lucky if you get out of it, and unlucky if you don't," I said.

"That's right," Gil said. "But I don't care to play Russian roulette."

Barry interrupted. "Anybody have a spoon they're not using?" Auten licked his off and passed it over to Barry, who thanked him.

"I think the ideal thing is to try relocating the camp," I said. "Try to put it on a rise instead of in a groove and it ought to be 98 or 99 per cent safe."

"Maybe," Dick conceded. "You've got to do some careful calculating on that whole area to find such a spot. You've got a potential avalanche slope above everything."

This did seem to be true. Gil ended the discussion:

"Whether you yourself are willing to camp there or not has nothing to do with it," he said. "The way I look at it, if you're going to use Sherpas, you're obligated to take care of them and protect them. And the way to protect them is not to put them in a camp at the bottom of an avalanche slope."

Willi didn't quite concede; he just changed the subject. But had he really believed what he was saying, or was he only debating?

Starting on a new tack, he said: "We've got to carry those two lousy winches on up to try them again. Obviously, Al's the guy who's got to do it, because he has the know-how to make them work." Looking at me, he added, "And obviously one of us two has to go up also."

"Why, obviously?" Dick asked.

"Because you guys are on R. and R., that's why," Willi answered. "You're run down and recuperating. And since Hornbein is under the weather . . ."

"I'm not under the weather."

"Just barely made it up here," Willi said.

"You had to run the corners, Unsoeld. We made it up in two and a half hours, almost a record."

"Just as long as you two compete with each other, I don't give a damn," Dick said.

Two days later, Willi and Al headed up with two spare winch motors and ether to prime them. They were determined to make them work. Eight Sherpas went up with them to carry the remainder of our supplies from the New Dump to Camp 3W. They would stay at 3W and descend each day to pick up loads.

The next three days were immaculate summit days, alas, with us nowhere near our destination and looking up eight thousand feet at that which had hung out of reach so long. One night we watched the full moon rise over the summit of Lhotse. Long before it appeared, the slopes above shone white as the shadow of Lhotse crept downward across the face of Everest. Ridges and flutings blocked the light, leaving swaths of impenetrable darkness in their lee. Night retreated up-Cwm before the steadily advancing light, and in its wake black slits of crevasses scored the gently rolling whiteness. Lhotse's skyline began to glow, caught fire from the eerie light, then disgorged a thin edge of unbelievable brightness. The moon burst from behind the mountain, taking possession of the knoll on which Dick and I stood. Bathed by light devoid of warmth, we shivered, reluctant to surrender the moment for the comfort of our beds. Undulating terraces of the Lhotse Glacier mirrored the brilliance of the moon. Fear lurked in the shadows, memory stirred.

Such weather couldn't last. On May 9 it snowed hard. Mindful of the avalanche hazard below 3W, we stayed put. The major consequence of the lost day became apparent at the radio contact with Base the following afternoon:

Advance Base (Gil Roberts): The feeling up here is that Bishop and Lute should postpone coming up by a day because the West Ridge is running a day behind and Lester wants to shrink them before they leave. Over.

Base (Prather): They're looking for a summit date of the 18th, possibly the 19th. They can't delay any more. When is the West Ridge planning a summit attempt? Over.

Advance Base (Roberts): The 20th.

Base (Prather): That's too late, and too bad! Barrel and Lute are going to just about have to go up tomorrow. Over.

Advance Base (Roberts): This means that they won't form any support for the West Ridge Party and people are wondering why!

Base (Prather): The porters are coming in on the 21st and we're leaving Base Camp on the 22d. Over.

Advance Base (Roberts): Basically, I'm not in the mood to get into the argument, because I don't really give a damn about it. Why don't you talk to Hornbein. Over.

Base (Prather): They just say they're coming up tomorrow. Over.

Advance Base (Hornbein): The only conditions under which we can hit the summit on the 19th or 20th are if we do not lose any more days because of weather. In other words, perfect conditions. Is this clear?

Base (Prather): Roger, Roger. Gotcha. It's just that time is running out. Over.

Advance Base (Hornbein): May I talk to Norman, please?

Base (Prather): Roger, he's listening. [Norman, with laryngitis, couldn't talk.] Go ahead.

Advance Base (Hornbein): O.K., we realize time is running out but we envisioned that there were a few more days beyond the 20th or 21st, so far as summit attempts by our route are concerned. And even though this might retard at least part of the exodus from Base Camp, we would hope that we could pursue our attempt beyond the 20th or 22d of May. How do you read that? Over.

Base (Prather): Only comment is, there are 300 porters coming in here on the 21st. Over.

Advance Base (Hornbein): Well, I guess we'll see you in Kathmandu then. Are we going to have any support for our traverse if we happen to get that far and it happens to be later than the 20th of May? Over.

Base (Barry Bishop): Tom, do you read me? Over.

Advance Base (Hornbein): Yes, I do, Barrel. Fire away.

Base (Bishop): Righto. Lute and I will delay another day, so that the first possibility of our hitting the summit will be the 19th and, if weather closes in, we may be able to give her a go on the 20th. But I think that's about it. How does that tie in with you, Tom?

Advance Base (Hornbein): As long as the weather is this good, fine. We lost yesterday because of tremendous snowfall and a fantastic avalanche hazard up there. We'll expect to see you here one day later. I would drop one other thought, though, that

NORMAN G. DYHRENFURTH: Lhotse, South Col, and Camp V, from Camp VI on Mount Everest

you consider leaving us a small nest egg if you really have to pull out on the 22d. In case we get out a little later than that, we can move out behind you and perhaps catch up. Over.

Base (Prather): Roger. We hope this doesn't happen, though.

I could understand Lute's and Barry's impatience. The longer they waited in order to synchronize with us the more they jeopardized their own summit opportunity. But if we chose to, or were forced by difficulties on the West Ridge to traverse the mountain and descend to the South Col, their presence would add greatly to our safety. Once again the question, what priority did the West Ridge have in the scheme of things? Why, now that the Col route was climbed, wasn't the decision made to wholeheartedly support our effort? Wasn't it our turn now?

On the following morning, the conversation resumed:

Base (Prather): Lute and Barrel don't want to delay too long. However, on the brighter side, we're going to delay leaving until the 25th. So go get her! Over.

Advance Base (Hornbein): Very good, Balu! We greatly appreciate the 25th.

Base (Dingman): One other thing, Tom. We're wondering, because of the oxygen situation on the Col, about the possibility of deciding now that the traverse is unfeasible. Do you read? Over.

Advance Base (Hornbein): I don't think we can make that decision, Dave. It's going to end up being a climbing decision, I suspect. If we can possibly traverse it might be the easiest way down. Over.

Base (Dingman): Roger, Tom. But you don't want to go over with no one in the Col.

Advance Base (Hornbein): I think that will depend on how hard it is getting down the other way. If there is no support, if at all possible, we would prefer to go down the way we came up, but I don't know that we can really answer this until we see how things work out.

The 11th was another lost day. The summit of Everest was capped by a seething black lenticular cloud. Rainbows flashed along its edge. The roar of wind against rock filled the Cwm. I sensed the uncontained power I could not see.

On May 12 I wrote: "Damn! We're falling behind, mostly discouraged with weather and lack of progress. This A.M., Norm, laryngitic-voiced, came on the radio to reaffirm the plan. Bishop and Lute could not wait for the summit beyond the 21st. Lute, Bishop, and Jim Whittaker all took the air to induce us not to try the traverse—too hazardous to descend a route unknown to us. Norm closed with heartiest good wishes for the success of our great and desperate undertaking, making me feel all warm inside. Eight more days could see us through. Whatever the outcome for me, the whole wealth of the Expedition, or much of it anyway, lies ahead. Without this prospect the affair to now would seem mighty unsatisfying and not a little sour—but horribly educational.

"Tomorrow, I'm up to 3W. Next day, to 4W, the following, a recon to 5W, and then we are moving."

Sketch by Mignon Linck, from the *American Alpine Journal,* 1964

12. A Blusterous Day

MAY 13 was a day for celebration. Thirty long frustrating days after our descent from the Reconnaissance, Camp 3W was finally stocked. I accompanied Willi and the last load of oxygen bottles up the slope late that afternoon as Al, not visible above, reigned supreme over the winch motor, nursing, begging, coercing. His virtuosity kept the motor running till this last load of eighteen bottles was hauled over the final edge. From a single tent the camp had grown to five four-man structures, housing a record population that night —fifteen Sherpas and three Sahibs. I was weary after the long haul up from Advance Base, but my communication to my diary was expectant: "3W again, at last!"

We had enough carrying power to afford some attrition, but not much. The Sherpas were tired. Many had carried to the South Col twice and several had been to Camp 6. Whether they were physically drained or whether they figured now that the mountain was climbed it was foolish to ask for more trouble, I don't know. Phu Dorje and Dawa Tenzing, two of the strong men on the Col route, turned back from the carry that Willi took to 4W. Before their lack of enthusiasm could infect the others, I sent them on down to Advance Base. Illness and inertia ran rampant, but were cured in part by Jimmy Roberts' voice over the radio promising extra pay: each carry beyond 3W would count on the wage scale as one camp higher than on the Col route. Our progress held to schedule.

On the afternoon of May 15, Willi and I moved up to 4W. We were alone with the grandeur that had captivated us that magical afternoon a month before. Wanting to shout my elation to those below I climbed onto the rock promontory, walkie-talkie in one hand and signal mirror in the other. I lay down on my belly at the edge of the precipice and tried to arouse someone at Advance Base, four thousand feet below. No one was outside. I waited a few minutes, then scooted gingerly back from the edge and returned to the tent. Its orange-yellow radiance in the afternoon sun was in garish contrast to the brown of barren hills rolling enigmatically onward beyond the North Col. Certainly there was no more fantastic place on the entire mountain, and it belonged to us!

But we were only guests, and the mountain proceeded to remind us of it, but with humor. It was 9 P.M. and diaries were finished. Tomorrow's water, two quarts of it, was melting on the stove as we prepared for an early start. Now, where did my plastic oxygen mask go? I groped through the innards of my sleeping bag; no mask. I emerged for my flashlight, then dove back in again. The glimmer of light penetrating the down bag caught Willi's attention.

"What are you doing in there?"

"Hunting for my mask. Had it in my hand a minute ago."

"Maybe it's under your bag."

Emerging, I turned on my knees and looked under the bag. No mask. Along the edge of the tent, under my air mattress— still no mask.

"Maybe it's in your bag, Willi. Take a look, will you?"

"How could it get in mine?"

"I don't know, but it's got to be somewhere." My exploratory gymnastics were becoming violent.

"Watch the water, Tom!"

I did—as my air mattress flipped the two quarts, won so hard, cleanly off the stove and sent them coursing down the groove between our air mattresses.

"What's that on your bag, Tom, behind you?"

There, innocently, lay my mask. I stared chagrined. This was too much. I wasn't about to begin melting more water tonight. Worry about that tomorrow. Since we were well above the high tide of what had spilled, it could darn well wait till morning too. When it froze we could pick it up and throw it out. I put on my sleeping mask, turning the regulator to one liter per minute.

"Night, Tom. You seem to be cracking under the strain. Maybe you'd better go down tomorrow."

"Drop dead, Unsoeld. Goodnight."

The next day was windy, not the sort on which you'd want to wander far from home, especially without water. Lethargically we melted more, and scraping up the frozen remainder of last night's catastrophe, tossed it out the door. By noon our reluctance to join the wind outside succumbed to boredom within. We decided to go as far as the Diagonal Ditch for a possible view across the North Face.

Unfortunately, from the top of the Ditch we couldn't see a thing.

"Let's go around one more corner," Willi said.

Curiosity and the deceptive foreshortening of distance on this vast face lured us on to unintentional fulfillment of our original plan. At 3:30 we sat down on the limestone slabs at the bottom of Hornbein's Couloir. Here, at the anticipated site of our next to last camp, the altimeter read 26,250 feet, a shade higher than the South Col. Above us the snow gully cut steeply up into the heart of the mountain, clear sailing for at least five hundred feet, then a slight bend obscured the view. Wind sent clouds of snow scurrying down the gully and momentarily blotted even the foreground from sight. Our traverse had been steep at times on rotten wind-slabbed snow. Crampons scraped across downsloping shingles of limestone. I felt haunted by history and thoughts of Mallory. Might we be near the point where he had walked? Where is he now?

Suspense lightly seasoned the journey back. Snow carried by the rising wind had obliterated our tracks and now limited our visibility to scarcely a rope length. On this slanting expanse it would be easy to become confused. But luck and an instinctive feeling for terrain acquired over many years of climbing homed us in on the rock castle that marked the top of the Diagonal Ditch. We reached 4W at 6 P.M., along with a lot more wind. During our absence the camp had grown. Behind our two-man tent were two four-man Drawtites, hooked together end-to-end.

Inside Barry, Al, and four Sherpas were eating.

"Hi, Barry, where's Emerson? Didn't he come up with you?"

"No. We started out from Advance Base together yesterday, but he was going so slow it was obvious that he'd never make it to 3W. He said something about trying again today."

At 7 P.M., Barry called Base.

Corbet (4W): Willi and Tom have located Camp 5 at 26,300 feet. The route to Camp 5 is good, the route above Camp 5 looks good. The West Ridge is on schedule. No further traffic. Over.

Prather (Base): Tremendous! Tremendous! Get some snow and soil samples for Will. Over.

Corbet (4W): Roger, Roger. All we have to do is hold the bottles up in the air and let the wind do the rest. Over.

Prather (Base): Norman and the whole gang down here say "Good deal on Camp 5W."

Bishop (Advance Base): Those of us here at 2 are jumping up and down. Good show! Get some sleep tonight in that heavy wind up there. One last thing—you'd better not count on Emerson from the way things are going. He's moving real slow. We can look up now and see he's just about at the New Dump, about three or four hours out at his present pace, and he said something about a possible bivouac on the way.

Prather (Base): Norman says here, and it's agreed, that Dick should not fiddle around any more up there. Dick should come down.

Bishop (Advance Base): Well, we'll have to wait till he gets to 3W and hope there's a radio.

But Dick was nowhere near a radio, or 3W.

"If I was strong," he wrote later, "I could have made it in a day, but I knew I would either have to bivouac enroute or arrive exhausted.

"Lute counseled me against exposing myself to frostbite in the bivouac. However, there was one bottle of oxygen and a convenient crevasse at what had been the New New Dump at a little over 23,000 feet. I had been down in the crevasse before, retrieving a fouled winch cable, and knew it to be suitable. If I slept on oxygen there would be no frostbite. Next day I started up, carrying an air mattress, which I concluded would be more useful than a sleeping bag. With the crevasse as my objective, I took a slow and steady pace and arrived at dusk feeling very well. I debated continuing the last 700 vertical feet to 3W, but it would be totally dark, and I was confident about the bivouac. In fact, I think I wanted the bivouac, but I don't know exactly why.

"It must have taken me almost two hours to get myself prepared for the night. I found the bottle half buried, put it in my pack, anchored a piece of rope to a picket, and rappeled into the dark hole as light was failing. About thirty feet down, the crevasse closed to four feet wide, plugged with powder snow. I tamped it firm, then started to inflate the mattress. I stopped. (Stupid, you'd better get those crampons off or you'll puncture it for sure.) As I fiddled with things in the dark, I could hear the wind rising. (No worry—but it's dumping a lot of snow in here.) I removed my down gloves to work with the oxygen gear. (Careful! Put the right glove in the right pocket—now left in left. Don't misplace one. Don't let snow sift into them. Hold the hose in your teeth. Now, work fast with the metal attach-

ments—hose to regulator, regulator to tank—keep the snow away and hope the threads seat well. Good, gloves. Now, down pants over the boots, wind shell, mask in place, regulator in reach. Flow? One liter. And now for sleep. Wait! Let's review: Where's my ax? Upright behind my head. Crampons? In the pack. Damn! I'll bet the flap's open. Goggles? Top left pocket.) This poor-man's countdown put my mind at ease and I drifted into sleep in perfect comfort, never suspecting the storm I was creating at Base Camp.

"Some time during the night I was awakened by cold around my eyes, where powder snow was sifting in. I was thoroughly warm otherwise, but slowly realized that I was totally buried. I rose to my feet, cradling the oxygen bottle like a baby in one arm. I pulled the mattress to the surface, remade my bed, and listening to the wind roaring past my cavern, immediately fell back to sleep."

Just after midnight that same evening Al unzipped the entrance to the yellow tent, stuck his head inside, and with effort roused Willi and me to report matter-of-factly, "A couple of tents just blew away."

Stupid with sleep, we mulled over his news, finally comprehending that the tents he, Barry, and the four Sherpas were in had got loose.

"We're about 150 feet down the hill," he said, "A real mess. I fixed them down as best I could, but you'd better check on them."

Fatigue imposed a strange detachment as Willi and I climbed into our boots and parkas. Leaving Al as ballast we stepped out into the staggering blast of the wind. Our headlights lit the swath planed by the sliding tents. Only then did we begin to appreciate the power of the storm, and imagine the horror of suddenly waking to find your tent sliding across the snow, accelerating in a headlong journey toward Tibet. By some miracle the tents had stopped in a shallow depression just below. Like surrealistic sculpture, their external frames were now a mass of contorted tubing from which the skin flapped noisily. The floor was uppermost. The end of Corbet's air mattress protruded from a hole in the side. There was a certain fatalistic humor in the voices within. Willi and I sank ice axes deep in the snow and proceeded to lash the wreckage to them with several lengths of climbing rope.

"All O.K.? Nawang? Everybody comfortable?" Willi called in.

"O.K. Sahib," came the reply.

"Lemunuk. Good job. Don't leave without us," he requested. Once the implications were understood, we were answered with good-humored laughter.

"See you in the morning, Barry. Keep cool," Willi said.

Leaning into the breeze, we plodded up the hill, fighting for breath every five or six steps. Eventually we poured in on Al, who was holding down the fort, and soon the three of us were sound asleep.

The sun touched the top of Everest before seven on May 17. Four thousand feet below, on the crest of a ridge sat our yellow-orange tent. Beaten nearly to submission, it clung to the mountainside. Roar of wind against the mountain served as background for the staccato vibration of the tent walls. Inside two of us sat hunched at the windward corners, leaning into the gale, convinced our effort was all that held our perch to the mountainside. The third enjoyed brief respite from the battering ordeal that had grown in intensity with the dawn. Above the sky was immaculately blue.

It was enough to give you a headache. I sat at the back corner, leaning into the pole, which obligingly had conformed to the curvature of my spine. My head was being riveted as if by a jackhammer. Al held the other corner, while Willi unfolded a grisly tale of another windstorm from his not forgotten youth. Half the story was lost in the racket of the tent walls. For the moment I found myself not terribly captivated anyway. The power unleashed upon us was frightening. What was there to keep it from sweeping us off the mountain? We were powerless to alter the scheme of things. It was humbling. I wondered briefly what I was doing here, what insanity had led me to become trapped in such a ridiculous endeavor. The thought was rapid, carthartic; anybody so stupid deserves to be in a place like this. Since you're here you might as well enjoy it, T., even Unsoeld's stories.

I looked at Al leaning silently against the other corner. His doubts were under control. And Willi's also. Or was he more talkative than usual? All three of us were certainly aware of our tenuous hold on the hillside, but what could we do besides make light of it?

At eight we called Base Camp on the radio. Corbet was already talking to Prather when we came on.

Corbet (*4W-lower site*): Let me fill you in. We've had a mishap during the night. Both Drawtite tents with the four Sherpas and Al and myself blew 150 feet down the slope and we're currently lying in a tangle of oxygen bottles. Al has gone up to join Willi and Tom, both of whom came down at midnight when it happened, and roped us to the slopes and I guess we're safe. We're currently waiting rescue by Willi and Tom and Al.

Unsoeld (*4W-upper site*): Can you read 4W now?

Prather (*Base*): I read you loud and clear, Willi. Did you get what Barry wanted?

Unsoeld (*4W*): I think I did. Yes, it's going to be a while yet, Bear, because we're just barely holding on to the Gerry tent. Here's a question, Bear; how's the wind down your way? Over.

Prather (*Base*): It's blowing a little bit down here, not very hard though—twenty or twenty-five miles per hour. Over.

Unsoeld (*4W*): I see. Well, we may not be able to hold out here much longer, Bear. Tent's taking a beating. Wind's blowing about a hundred pretty steady. Over.

Prather (*Base*): We can see a hell of a lot of wind coming off Nuptse and it really sounds bad. There's a big roar we can hear, from down here even. Over.

Unsoeld (*4W*): I can believe it. Over.

Our growing concern over Dick's whereabouts was relieved when Dingman came on.

Dingman (*Advance Base*): Willi, did you hear about Emerson? Over.

Unsoeld (*4W*): No I didn't, Dave. What's the latest word? Over.

Dingman (*Advance Base*): We looked out of the tent a few minutes ago and lo and behold, we saw him between the New Dump and the crest, still going up. Over.

Unsoeld (*4W*): Did I get that right? You saw him between the New Dump and the crest and he was going up? Over.

Dingman (*Advance Base*): Roger.

Unsoeld (*4W*): And that was *this* morning? Over.

Prather (*Base*): Roger, that's this morning, just a few minutes ago. Over.

Unsoeld (*4W*): Holy Cow! I can't believe it! Over.

Prather (*Base*): Roger. You're not the only one.

Unsoeld (*4W*): That's great news, Dave! Great news! Now if we can get out of this mess, we'll be fine. Over.

Well protected in his fastidiously prepared hole, Dick had hibernated peacefully through the night, oblivious of the storm above. He described what took place when he woke for the second time:

"Soft light filled the crevasse, but I couldn't see the opening above me for the swirling snow. My watch said 7:00, but the light suggested 4:00 (Radio contact is at 8:15. Get on your way again by then so they can see you from Camp 2 and know all is well. But no rush now.) So I lay there marveling at the comfort of such a form-fitting bed, watching the snow sweep by above me with unbelievable velocity.

"Eventually I rose and started putting things in shape. (Will the weather block visibility from Camp 2?) I pulled the plug to let the mattress deflate and found that it had frozen up when only half-deflated. I rolled it up under my pack flap and, using the front points of my crampons, started up the rappel rope to rejoin the elements.

"It was 8:45, the sky was blue, and I could see the tents at 2 far below, yet I couldn't see my own feet in the blowing snow. I started up the home stretch for 3W, wondering if I could be seen in the ground blizzard. My route went straight up the 35° slope, scoured hard by the cross-wind. Once, standing erect to see over the turmoil of moving particles, I was hit like a hammer by a wind change and did a self-arrest moving horizontally across the slope. I continued steadily on front points and a pick. Soon, snow filtering through the air vents filled my goggles. Since there was no feasible way to clean them, nor any point in doing so, I put them away and continued, squinting out through the wolverine fur of my hood. All I had to do was go straight up. I didn't have to see. The wind tore the partly inflated mattress from my pack and I last saw it gaining altitude westward."

About nine, Barry crept up the slope to join us. The four Sherpas had headed down to 3W. We felt sure such tremendous power must soon spend itself, but nothing in the behavior of the wind lent support to our wishful thinking. Momentary lulls left the tent walls hanging limp; the sudden staccatoless silence was filled by the roar of the wind across the ridge above. Was the storm subsiding? In seconds the answer came, unnecessarily malicious in its suddenness. The tent strained against its anchors in response to a blast that had gained strength in its momentary pause for breath. Then there was just more roar. We decided to retreat while there was still something to retreat from. Al headed out on his hands and knees in search of his rucksack. His concern for something so inconsequential seemed strange.

At Base Camp the crew sat comfortably about the breakfast table sipping tea, listening to the radio set in the corner of the tent.

Dingman (Advance Base): Have you got the weather forecast?

Prather (Base): Yes. Just a second here. Forecast is generally cloudy with strong winds and a few snow showers likely. The outlook, a low pressure area is now over Punjab, the one that was over Afghanistan, and may affect us in about forty-eight hours. Over.

Unsoeld (4W): Four to Base. Four to Base. Over.

Prather (Base): Roger, Willi. Reading you loud and clear. Go ahead.

Unsoeld (4W): O.K. Here's the latest report, Bear. (Suddenly the tent began to slide.) O-o-v-e-e-r-r-r!

Prather (Base): You want the weather report? Over.

Unsoeld (4W): God damn! The tent's blowing away!

Prather (Base): Roger. The tent's blowing away. We'll stand by.

Unsoeld (4W): Stand by. We're headed over the brink!

Prather (Base): Roger.

Unsoeld (4W): Barry! Out! Out!

Nearest the door, I shucked my mitts, and dove for the zippers, ripping them down. Happily they didn't jam. As we gained speed, I shot from the tent. A metal rappel picket was lying on the snow. I rammed it in, spreading my legs in the vestibule, and held tight. The tent stopped. Barry emerged. "What do we do now, Tom?" he asked, and as I thought, he piled oxygen bottles on the structure to complete what little remained of the final flattening process. I turned to see Willi, hunched low before the wind, still talking on the radio.

Unsoeld (4W): Well, we're all out, the tent's gone, and we're headed for 3 as fast as possible. Over.

Leaning into the blast, the four of us staggered down to retrieve our axes which held the lower tents to the slope.

Suddenly the wind caught the wreckage, whipping it about with a frenzy that threatened to sweep Barry off the mountain. We shouted at him to get away, but he couldn't possibly have heard. A box of food skidded over the snow bound for the depths of the Rongbuk. A sleeping bag shot from a rent in the fabric and, inflating like a giant green windsock, flew upward to disappear into the wall of blowing snow.

Unroped we were blown stumbling and falling the remaining distance to the shelter of the ridge behind the crest. There we could stand erect, but now the wind came in gusts from every direction. Ground blizzard obscured the track. Snow stung my face like flying sand and filtered in to cake the inside of my goggles. I couldn't see a thing. Where'd Willi disappear to? A gust jarred me from the track and I dropped about six feet down a wall. From somewhere Willi appeared and looked down as if to ask, What are you doing there, Tom?

It seemed an eternity before we reached the border, crossed over, and started down the other side out of the wind. Only then was there time to think about what had happened. I sat in the snow a hundred feet above the tents to wait, not sure whether Willi was hanging back out of sheer fatigue or for a bit of aloneness. After a while, he trudged slowly into view and settled down beside me. He was tired. The wind-sculptured ice on his face was like the frost feathers in winter on timberline trees back in the Northwest. The frozen extension of his nose held a strange fascination, enough for me to overcome fatigue and bring out my camera.

As we sat there, the realization came that we were finished, demolished, literally blasted off the mountain. We hadn't even sunk our teeth solidly into the climb. I felt no gratitude that we had escaped with our lives, only awe at the power unleashed on us, and a dissatisfied feeling of finality to all our dreams. After a while we struggled to our feet and wobbled wearily down to the tents at 3W.

. . . For it is a strange fact, but one that has always proved true, that where one man has imposed his domination over the elements another man can pass. The way is open, because the forces of nature have waited for man to prove himself master before submitting. A poor, puny, lonely master, but always since the day when he ate of the fruit of the tree of knowledge animated by the will to take possession of the mysteries. And the gigantic and inflexible forces become blunted. One man prepares the terrain for another man; everywhere, in every field of endeavor, the inaccessible and the impossible are only a matter of great patience, a patience which man has within him, not as his own property (in fact, failure deprives him of the benefits of his patience) but as a magic ring which the vanquished gives to him who succeeds in the attempt. Thus, in the long run, the gates open which man at first believed to be remorselessly closed.

—RENÉ DITTERT

13. Severing the Cord

WE WERE stacked irresolutely about the tent: Barry, Al, Willi, Ang Dorje, Dick, and I. Dick appeared none the worse for his night out. It was hard to regret that we were beaten, so enticing was the prospect of fresh meat and unlimited eggs awaiting us at Base Camp, and the prospect of our homeward journey. To be off this mountain once and for all was the only goal with any meaning. We would have continued down to Advance Base that same day, but we were too tired. We crawled into our bags that night with the feeling that it was all over. The prospect of escaping from this inhospitable lump that could out of sheer whimsy blot us neatly from the scheme of things was pure delight. The lure of home was stronger still, the welling-up of love and longing. And strongest of all was the prospect of finally being freed from the lure of the mountain. The invisible line that linked me to Everest was frayed.

But it hadn't broken. I wasn't yet free to make my own decision. We hadn't given it all we had. Descend now, and we must live the rest of our lives with that knowledge. So the bond still held fast. But it would be sheer fanaticism to suggest going back up. Weary muscles voted against the taunting of my mind; still I couldn't shake it off. Our tents were ruined, a lot of food blown away. And oxygen? Four Sherpas had beat a hasty retreat to Advance Base. Three days ago we had fifteen, now only three remained, Ang Dorje, Passang Tendi, and Tenzing Nindra. We could salvage two four-man tents from here. Maybe we could get a small one from Advance Base. And a couple more Sherpas. But time was running out. We were scheduled to leave Base in a week.

Months before, in our early planning we had toyed with the idea of having only five camps, instead of six as on the Col. It would cut down the number of carries high on the mountain over terrain few of our Sherpas would be skilled enough to climb. The idea was ridiculous. How could we hope to travel farther in a day over steep, difficult terrain than on the easier ground of the regular route? We discarded the idea as naïve folly. We'd need at least six camps. Two two-man summit teams on successive days went without saying.

We had been hamstrung by the wind, and new questions kept me awake: Can we possibly consider going up? Suppose we eliminate a camp and try for a very long carry above 4W? A long shot, but it's the only chance we have. Over two thousand vertical feet in a day? Maybe, if the climbing isn't too tough and the loads are light. If we can get two more Sherpas, that'll still be forty pounds apiece—for just one summit team. There isn't time for a second one anyway. No time to send our recon a day early to locate the high camp. They'll just have to get up early and hope the going is not too hard.

So we have a chance. If the Sherpas will agree to one more carry. It's worth a try. I was bursting to tell my plan to Willi. With the dawn I could contain myself no longer. I kneed him in the ribs.

"Excuse me. I didn't mean to wake you up. But since you are, what do you think of this?"

Willi forced open a sleepy eye and listened, wondering whether what he heard was sheer genius or only my pathological fanatacism. Undoubtedly the latter, he must have thought, but still it was a chance.

"O.K. Let's try it on Barry."

Barry bit. We crossed to the other tent and accosted Dick and Al. And so it was agreed. We called Base on the radio and Willi presented our plan.

Dyhrenfurth (Base): Willi, I'm delighted by your plan. This is exactly what we were going to suggest, that only two men make the attempt. And all I can say is, Willi, you've had a hell of a lot of tough luck. You've worked awfully hard. And we're all 200 percent with you. We wish you all the luck in the world and hope you make it. Over.

Unsoeld (3W): Thanks a lot, Norm. We appreciate that and I'm especially appreciative that we're thinking along the same lines. Really, this is probably a terrifically long shot. If we can carry through to 27,000 or so and then have to retreat we would all feel as if we had completed an adequate reconnaissance of the route. With 90 per cent of the labor already done getting the things up to 4W it seems too bad to come down without one last all-out push, which, with a little bit of luck, we'll carry out. Thanks a lot, Norm. Over.

Dyhrenfurth (Base): Willi, we all thank God, of course, that you are all alive, that nobody got hurt, and whether you make it or not, in any case you have accomplished miracles. I think the mountaineering world, I'm sure, will recognize that this is an incredible accomplishment on a long and difficult and unknown route. Over.

Willi (3W): Thanks a lot. We share your joy in all being alive, all right. There were a few times when things were flying around wildly that we weren't sure but that some of the objects were us. And, I don't know, if we just get one break in the weather now, it's entirely possible to go all the way. The Couloir really looks good. The section of it that Tom and I were in looked like it was the steepest of all that we could see and it was a maximum of thirty to thirty-five degrees. So it didn't look like a difficult route as far as we could see. The upper part of the mountain might give us something we can really sink our teeth in. Over.

Dyhrenfurth (Base): Willi, it sounds very, very good. All the luck in the world. As they say in German, *Hals und Beinbruch.* Over.

Al took to the air to consult Prather about replacing gear lost in the storm.

Auten (3W): We'll need a couple of packs. Mine and Barry's took off and are somewhere in China by now. Also two pairs of goggles, and two of down mitts. Hornbein says he needs some Bouton goggles, too, and a balaclava. And Jimmy's two-man Gerry tent at Advance Base if he can give it up.

Prather (Base): Mighty fine. Big Jim sends good word up to you. He's sending his pack up to you, and he says that the pack's been to the summit. It's a very expensive pack. And he says if you lose his pack your soul had better go to Heaven because your ass will be his. Over.

We were completely on our own. For all the wellwishing we knew the impatience of those below to be homeward bound. They knew our chances were slim; it was kindness that they still waited. I guess they also knew we wouldn't come down until we were damned well through. We had kept the ridge attempt alive against an opposition which we thought was founded on doubt and lack of interest. Though hardly burdened with manpower or supplies, we were finally in position.

We rested the next two days, and waited for supplies. On the first morning Al wanted to go down. He had worked hard and well, but only a little of our enthusiasm for the route had rubbed off on him. Now he could see Dick assuming his original role in the foursome, with himself as excess baggage. I protested.

"We need all the manpower we can get," I said. "Dick's strength is still a big question and any one of the rest of us could wake up sick tomorrow. Let's not cut it any thinner than it is already. We need you."

Al stayed.

The 18th and 19th were perfectly clear. Our colorful down clothes bloomed atop the tents. The summit of Everest stood a mile above, windless and inviting. The afternoon of the 19th, Ila Tsering and Tenzing Gyaltso arrived, all smiles, with our fresh supplies. Our discussion that afternoon went once more over the final plans. Till now we had not decided on the final route. Hornbein's Couloir lay far out on the Tibetan North Face, almost in a fall line below the summit; Jake's was a large snowfield leading back up toward the West Ridge. We were drawn toward the latter, because it would return us to the Ridge we had meant to climb. But we no longer had the strength to move a camp up that kind of terrain. We had to get it above 27,000 feet in the easiest way possible. With time for but one long carry, Hornbein's Couloir appeared to offer us the only chance. Where the Couloir went, above the camp, we couldn't guess. We'd just have to take our chances on the final day.

Dick broached the last unaired issue.

"I'd think in all fairness we ought to discuss the choice of the summit team. I don't mind being outspoken since I'm not in shape for it anyway. There's no question that Barry, Tom, and Willi are in the best shape. I think this is the first consideration."

We weighed the various pairings.

"I think Willi and Tom should go," Barry said. "For one thing, you've plugged harder on the route than any of the rest of us."

"All the more reason for you to have a turn, Barry," Willi replied.

In the six weeks we'd been on the mountain, Barry had not tasted a day of real climbing, of pushing a route over new terrain. He'd spent his time humping loads and toiling over the winch, or sitting restlessly at Advance Base. Though he said little, his frustration and disappointment were apparent. He

had discovered that there wasn't much real climbing involved in climbing the highest peaks on earth. He was a superb mountaineer. He could have easily gone to the top.

"Another thing," Corbet continued, "you two have been climbing together; you know each other, and you'll make the strongest team. What's more, you're both just about over the hump. This is my first expedition. I'll be coming back again someday."

So tentatively Willi and I were to be the summit team. The final decision would be made at our high camp two days later. If either of us fell out, Barry would plug the hole. We tackled the final problem in our tent that night. Barry would reconnoiter to find high camp. We had to decide who would accompany him. They'd have to start early and move fast to find and prepare a route for those following a few hours later. Dick had still not fully recovered from his illness. We doubted he could hold the pace. All things considered, it was decided that Al would go with Barry.

May 20 was the third perfect day in a row. How long could the weather hold? We struck the two tents that were to go to 4W. The snow had drifted level with their flat tops on the uphill side. Then the warmth from inside had caused a layer of ice to form. They were solidly imbedded. Much chopping finally extracted the tents with only a few additional holes for better ventilation. Willi and I sorted personal gear, some to stay at 4W, some to go up. A few pages were torn from the back of our diaries so that Emerson's study could continue uninterrupted without our having to carry the entire books over the summit. Shortly after noon we saddled up, set our oxygen at two liters per minute, and headed for the West Shoulder. The two days' rest had worked wonders.

Thinking of the possible traverse of Everest I said, "You know, Willi, if we're really lucky this may be the last time we see 3W." We both must have shared the next thought: Yes; and also if we're unlucky.

As we approached the Shoulder we could see the prayer flag Ang Dorje had planted there, flapping in the wind. Like a couple of proud children about to reveal their most treasured hideaway, we watched Dick come over the top for his first view of the other side. His silence as he looked was all we needed to make the moment perfect. We pointed out the landmarks of our route, so far as it went.

As Dick began to photograph the route, Willi remembered leaving his haze filter in my rucksack at 3W. Deciding that such picture-taking opportunities might not come his way again, he left his pack and headed back down. The others moved on up toward 4W to begin the salvage job while I waited on the crest of the ridge for Willi.

For almost the first time during the entire expedition I was completely alone. I sat atop the ridge with my mittens off, soaking up the windless warmth of the afternoon sun. I looked across brown hills, deep glacial valleys, snow peaks ranging westward into haze. My thoughts knew only the restriction imposed by the limits of my ability to feel and comprehend. A vertical mile above, at the far end of the West Ridge, was the highest point on earth. The day after tomorrow? The dream of childhood, not to be lost? My gaze climbed lightly up each detail of our route, to the base of the Couloir at 26,000 feet. The rest was unknown, partly hidden, grossly foreshortened, but all there.

Like pain, a mountain can be a subjective sensation; for all its solidity and fixity of form, it is more than what one sees. It is awe, pleasure, respect, love, fear, and much, much more. It is an ever-changing, maturing feeling. Over the weeks since we had first stood on the Shoulder to see the black rock of the last four thousand feet, my feelings toward the climb had steadily ripened. That rock couldn't be divorced from the summit to which it led. Yet each time we looked, the slope seemed a few degrees gentler, the vertical distance not quite so unreasonable. After all, we had climbed steeper faces and longer distances, and on more rotten rock. But all together? And above 27,000 feet instead of half that high? However, you can't see altitude. Might as well ignore it. We chose not to dwell on problems like what happens if you run out of oxygen below the summit. And what it's like to climb on rotten rock at 27,000 feet, ballasted by a forty-pound pack.

Everest came down off Everest. It became, in a climbing sense, just another mountain to be approached and attempted within the context of our past experience in the Rockies, Tetons, or on Mount Rainier. Not quite, really. But much of the battle lay inside. That battle was nearly won.

I looked out beyond the Great Couloir to the step where Mallory and Irvine were last seen. So near the Everest of my boyhood, I felt uneasy, as if I were trespassing on hallowed ground. I looked on the same North Face at which they had looked forty years before; I felt what they must have felt. The past was part of the rightness of our route.

Beyond the remains of the Rongbuk Monastery were the barren hills of Tibet, a strange land of strange people, living beneath the highest mountain on earth—did they know it? What difference did it make to them? I thought of home. It would be night there, everyone asleep. Can Gene feel my thoughts coming home? I took my photo album from my shirt pocket, and looked at the portraits inside. Tears came. Sheer, happy loneliness, the feeling of being nearly finished with the task I had set myself. It wouldn't be long now.

Completely alone. Range on range hazed westward. Beneath me clouds drifted over the Lho La, chasing their shadows across the flat of the Rongbuk Glacier. I remembered afternoons of my childhood when I watched the changing shapes of clouds against a deep blue sky, seeing elephants and horses and soft mountains. On this lonely ridge I was part of all I saw, a single, feeble heartbeat in the span of time and space about me.

Willi was back. He came steaming up the hill on full flow from a cylinder strapped to his back, his haze filter clutched in one hand. He checked his watch to confirm what undoubtedly must stand as a world's record for the run from 3W to the West Shoulder. Once he had caught his breath we took one last look at the sweep of mountain above us; henceforth we would be too much a part of it, able to locate ourselves only in the memory of this last soaring view. Squandering oxygen, we pressed the pace to join the others in rehabilitating the wreckage of 4W. Most of the oxygen bottles were still there, and enough butane if we used it carefully. But of twelve food boxes only three remained. One, fortunately, contained our high-camp ration. As Barry busily filmed us we began to pitch the tents. Four days before we had been forcibly made aware of the reason for our flat campsite, but there was no place else to put it. We oriented the two four-man tents with their broadsides less exposed to any recurrence of storm. The walls flapped disconcertingly in the westerly breeze. Al carefully enmeshed the cluster with climbing ropes.

The remnant of our original two-man tent was suspended from the frame of one of the larger tents; its own poles had been bent beyond repair. This sagging structure was to be Barry's and Dick's. Al would share one of the big tents with Ang Dorje and Tenzing Gyaltso. Feeling isolated, Al objected. Reluctantly the Sherpas consented to inhabit the ruined tent. They straightaway crawled inside and refused to come out for supper.

And up on the mountain we began our ant-like labours. What is a man on an ice-world up in the sky? At that altitude he is no more than a will straining in a spent machine. The farther he mounts the worse he breathes: his legs become powerless or rather foreign, as if they belonged to him no more, and he learns that the most steadfast energy is limited in action. Often, at the end of his tether, he sinks down into the snow without further thought, or more often he stops, bowing to the slope over his ice-axe, to try and recover his wind. He is loathe to move, but suddenly the spirit springs erect and orders the flesh to get up, to go on. Then once again the breath is short and the carcass comes to a halt.

The mountaineer sets off promising himself to regulate his pace carefully to his breathing: however he soon lacks air, for the air is so poor that it no longer feeds the machine. Nevertheless, step by step, the man stamps out the track, and if he looks over his shoulder he knows an instant of happiness: since his last halt he has gained a few score yards. Below him the Base Camp diminishes and grows distant. He feels isolated from the world of men, but the near presence of his comrade on the rope comforts him. Towards 23,000 feet life grows thinner still, is no more than an obsession: take a step, then another.

Only on the summit can we straighten our bodies that lean always uphill.

—GASTON REBUFFAT

"Not hungry, Sahib," said Ang Dorje, "only need sleep. O.K. tomorrow."

But we wondered how much they were offended. Knowing the highs and lows of their temperament, we worried that they might remain in bed "sick" in the morning. I crawled into their tent to rig their sleeping oxygen and try to persuade them to have some tea. Later Willi went over through the cold of the night to chat with Ang Dorje.

Our plans for May 21 seemed a little ridiculous. First, Barry and Al had to explore and prepare an unknown route to the site for our high camp, 5W. We would give them a 2½-hour head-start. Next, five untried Sherpas must traverse the North Face, climbing more than two thousand vertical feet with loads, twice the distance ever carried before at that altitude.

In the bitter, pre-sun cold, Al and Barry departed. They carried fixed rope, pitons, ice screws, and one oxygen cylinder each. They also carried all our hopes for the following day. After breakfast Dick, Willi, and I prepared the loads for the Sherpas. I checked the pressure in all the oxygen cylinders, setting aside the six fullest for the final push. By nine the sun was warming the tents, but there was still no sign of Ang Dorje and Tenzing Gyaltso. We began to consider seriously the consequences should they not show, when a smiling face appeared at their tent door.

"Good morning, Sahibs. Ready go," Ang Dorje said.

Ila Tsering looked over at Ang Dorje, supposedly past his prime but somehow totally infected with the pleasure of our gamble, then at the three other young Sherpas, all on their first expedition.

"All good Sherpas Base Camp, Sahib. Only bad Sherpas up here," he said.

Delighted laughter, theirs and ours, got us on our way. Each shouldered a load of about forty pounds, counting the oxygen he would use during the day. Ila hefted his load.

"Very heavy, Sahib," he said.

We took turns lifting it. Sure enough, our food ration weighed about ten pounds more than the other loads. He grinned. "But this last day," he said. "I carry."

At 9:30 the five Sherpas were roped together. I checked their masks as they filed past and set their regulators at a flow of 1½ liters per minute. They followed Barry and Al's tracks toward the Diagonal Ditch. Twenty minutes later Willi, Dick, and I pulled out. Willi and I carried only a single bottle of oxygen, cameras, radio, flashlight, and our personal belongings.

The Sherpas stayed one jump ahead. The three of us were completely absorbed in the pleasure of climbing together for the first time since Masherbrum. Since our visit five days before, the slope had changed radically. Entire snowfields had been blasted into oblivion, leaving us to scrape our crampons across an abundance of downsloping, fractured rubble. Far ahead we could see the figures of Barry and Al silhouetted against the snow as they disappeared into Hornbein's Couloir.

For me, the pleasure of the walk was tempered by anxiety. Could Al and Barry get to 27,500?

It was early afternoon before we reached the base of the Couloir, at 26,250 feet. Showers of ice cascading from above drew our attention to the tiny figures etched against the snow

eight hundred feet higher. Barry was chopping away for all he was worth, hewing a staircase for us. We joined the Sherpas under a partly protected wall to await the end of the onslaught and nibble a bit of lunch. The Sherpas seemed less enthusiastic as they huddled to avoid the constant bombardment of ice spewing out the end of the gully and whirring past our heads with a high-pitched whine. We dallied over our sardines, pineapple, and chocolate, all frozen tasteless. The prospect of entering the gully was too much like becoming tenpins in a high-angle bowling alley.

A little after 2 P.M. the ice fall abated. With Ang Dorje paternally in the lead, the Sherpas started up, their flow increased to 3 liters per minute. Dick had reached this select 8,000-meter level with little difficulty. He would have liked to go higher, but it seemed more sensible for him to remain here, conserving his energy and oxygen to assist the others on their late return to 4W. Our masks could not hide tears when it came time to head on up.

"Must be the altitude," said Willi.

"Don't do anything foolish, you nuts," Dick said. Then, as an afterthought, with a twinkle in his eye, "See you back at 2."

For a long time as we climbed we could look down on the back of Dick's head as he sat on that lonely ledge, looking out into Tibet.

The shadows were lengthening across the glaciers twelve thousand feet below. It was nearly 4 P.M. when we looked up to see Al and Barry, their two heads peering gnomelike from a snow ledge at the base of the Yellow Band. We shouted encouragement to the Sherpas, now below us, for they were beginning to suspect their Sahibs of wanting to pitch the last camp on the summit itself. The slope of the staircase Barry had carved steepened to about forty degrees as we came up to them. He filmed our arrival.

"O.K. Willi, come up around the end and turn toward me, and smile."

Willi smiled beneath his oxygen mask. My first breathless question as I reached the ledge was, "How high are we, Barry?"

"The altimeter says 27,200 and it's still rising."

"Wow! Tremendous. You guys did it!"

We'd have a long day tomorrow—but it was possible.

Willi had been hastily surveying their choice of a campsite. It was a wind-scooped depression running beneath the cliff for about ten feet. At the wide end it might have been twelve inches across.

"Where'd you find such spacious accommodations?" he asked.

"We knew you'd be satisfied with nothing but the best," Barry said, "but it's the only possibility we've seen all afternoon. Anyway you'll be able to keep warm digging a platform when we leave. Only please don't knock any ice down on us."

With the Sherpas clinging to the slope by their axes, we hacked out a hasty ledge, then gingerly passed the tent, food, and oxygen bottles up to it.

"Careful. If we lose a bottle of oxygen we're through."

It would be dark before they reached 4W. Again tears came as we thanked Ang Dorje, Ila, the two Tenzings, and Passang Tendi. "Good luck, Sahib," each one said as we clasped hands. Then we said goodbye to Barry. And to Al. Barry sank his ax into the snow to anchor the rope. Al led off, followed by the Sherpas. They slid quickly down the fixed line. Then Barry pulled his ax, descended carefully to them and repeated the process.

"Just like guiding Mount Owen, Willi," he shouted up.

There was only a brief moment to feel the grandeur of our impending isolation. We had to contrive some architectural plan for carving a tent platform from an excessively steep slope of snow.

"How about parallel to the cliff," I asked.

"I think it'll take less digging if we diagonal it out into the gully."

For the next hour and a half we chopped, jumping on the pieces to pulverize them to a size less painful should they accidently be launched onto the party descending below. Every effort was breathtakingly slow.

"Think it's big enough?" Willi asked.

"Let's give it a try."

With the wind threatening to blow it away, we pitched the tent.

"Nope. Not quite big enough. It seems to hang over a bit on the outside," I said. The platform was a good foot too narrow.

"How much do you weigh, Tom, boy?"

"About 130, stripped. Why?"

"I have you by twenty-five pounds. Maybe you better sleep on the outside."

I climbed in to start supper while Willi secured the tent to the slope. One rock piton driven half an inch into the rotten rock of the Yellow Band anchored the uphill ties, our axes buried to the hilt in equally rotten snow pinned the outside corners.

Willi ceremoniously planted the prayer flag Ang Dorje had left. "I think we'd better count on this," he said.

It promised to be a classical high-camp night on Everest: wind batters the tent while its occupants cling to the poles inside, sipping a cold cup of meager tea. We had the wind, the insecure platform—and the enticing prospect of a two-mile vertical ride into Tibet if our tent let go. But these modern tents had the poles on the outside; there was nothing to cling to. We turned to our meager fare. This began with chicken-rice soup, followed by a main course of butter-fried, freeze-dried shrimp in a curried tomato sauce, crackers and blackberry jam,

and a can of grapefruit segments for dessert. All this was interspersed with many cups of steaming bouillon. Our greatest sorrow was that we could do away with only two-thirds of the four-man luxury ration. We turned to a bit of oxygen as a chaser; once again we had overeaten.

Everything was readied for an early start. For this one night I succumbed to Unsoeld's slovenly habit of sleeping fully clothed, except for boots, which were the foundation under the outer half of my air mattress. While Willi stacked the oxygen bottles in the vestibule, I melted snow for tomorrow's water. This and the butane stoves would share the warmth of our sleeping bags to prevent their freezing during the night.

About nine Willi awoke from his after-dinner nap, gripped by an overwhelming urge to relieve himself which had for some time been overwhelming me. I promptly encouraged his leaving the tent by offering him a belay.

"No thanks, Tom. A guide can handle these things himself."

He disappeared into the gusty blackness, his flashlight inscribing chaotic circles of light. What a horrible way to go, I thought. And he has the flashlight!

After a time he returned, triumphant. We finished the evening religiously filling out Emerson's diary. Once more violating the classical Everest tradition, we turned our sleeping oxygen to one liter each and settled into the humidity of our plastic sleeping masks. To the lullaby of the wind shaking our high and lonely dwelling, we fell into a deep sleep. But just before that I wrote a letter home, without oxygen:

May 21
Camp 5W, 27,200

GENIE:

Just a brief note on our hopeful summit eve. 9:00 P.M. Willi and I perched in a hacked-out platform at the base of the Yellow Band in Hornbein's Couloir. The morrow greets us with 2,000 feet to the top, the first of which looks like some good rock climbing. Very breathless without oxygen. Mainly, as wind rattles the tent and I hang slightly over the edge, would have you know I love you. Tomorrow shall spell the conclusion to our effort, one way or another.

Good night.

Love always,
TOM

BETSY HORNBEIN: Tom on Mount Everest, May 1963 (sketch)

14. Promises to Keep...

AT FOUR the oxygen ran out, a most effective alarm clock. Two well-incubated butane stoves were fished from inside our sleeping bags and soon bouillon was brewing in the kitchen. Climbing into boots was a breathless challenge to balance in our close quarters. Then overboots, and crampons.

"Crampons, in the tent?"

"Sure," I replied, "It's a hell of a lot colder out there."

"But our air mattresses!"

"Just be careful. We may not be back here again, anyway. I hope."

We were clothed in multilayer warmth. The fishnet underwear next to our skin provided tiny air pockets to hold our body heat. It also kept the outer layers at a distance which, considering our weeks without a bath, was respectful. Next came Duofold underwear, a wool shirt, down underwear tops and bottoms, wool climbing pants, and a lightweight wind parka. In spite of the cold our down parkas would be too bulky for difficult climbing, so we used them to insulate two quarts of hot lemonade, hoping they might remain unfrozen long enough to drink during the climb. Inside the felt inner liners of our reindeer-hair boots were innersoles and two pairs of heavy wool socks. Down shells covered a pair of wool mittens. Over our oxygen helmets we wore wool balaclavas and our parka hoods. The down parka-lemonade muff was stuffed into our packs as padding between the two oxygen bottles. With camera, radio, flashlight, and sundry mementos (including the pages from Emerson's diary), our loads came close to forty pounds. For all the prior evening's planning it was more than two hours before we emerged.

I snugged a bowline about my waist, feeling satisfaction at the ease with which the knot fell together beneath heavily mittened hands. This was part of the ritual, experienced innumerable times before. With it came a feeling of security, not from the protection provided by the rope joining Willi and me, but from my being able to relegate these cold gray brooding forbidding walls, so high in such an unknown world, to common reality—to all those times I had ever tied into a rope before: with warm hands while I stood at the base of sun-baked granite walls in the Tetons, with cold hands on a winter night while I prepared to tackle my first steep ice on Longs Peak. This knot tied me to the past, to experiences known, to difficulties faced and overcome. To tie it here in this lonely morning on Everest brought my venture into context with the known, with that which man might do. To weave the knot so smoothly with clumsily mittened hands was to assert my confidence, to assert some competence in the face of the waiting rock, to accept the challenge.

Hooking our masks in place we bade a slightly regretful goodbye to our tent, sleeping bags, and the extra supply of food we hadn't been able to eat. Willi was at the edge of the ledge looking up the narrow gully when I joined him.

"My oxygen's hissing, Tom, even with the regulator turned off."

For the next twenty minutes we screwed and unscrewed regulators, checked valves for ice, to no avail. The hiss continued. We guessed it must be in the valve, and thought of going back to the tent for the spare bottle, but the impatient feeling that time was more important kept us from retracing those forty feet.

"It doesn't sound too bad," I said. "Let's just keep an eye on the pressure. Besides if you run out we can hook up the sleeping T and extra tubing and both climb on one bottle." Willi envisioned the two of us climbing Everest in lockstep, wed by six feet of rubber hose.

We turned to the climb. It was ten minutes to seven. Willi led off. Three years before in a tent high on Masherbrum he had expounded on the importance of knee-to-toe distance for step-kicking up steep snow. Now his anatomical advantage determined the order of things as he put his theory to the test. Right away we found it was going to be difficult. The Couloir, as it cut through the Yellow Band, narrowed to ten or fifteen feet and steepened to fifty degrees. The snow was hard, too hard to kick steps in, but not hard enough to hold crampons; they slid disconcertingly down through this wind-sheltered, granular stuff. There was nothing for it but to cut steps, zigzagging back and forth across the gully, occasionally finding a bit of rock along the side up which we could scramble. We were forced to climb one at a time with psychological belays from axes thrust a few inches into the snow. Our regulators were set to deliver two liters of oxygen per minute, half the optimal flow for this altitude. We turned them off when we were belaying to conserve the precious gas, though we knew that the belayer should always be at peak alertness in case of a fall.

We crept along. My God, I thought, we'll never get there at this rate. But that's as far as the thought ever got. Willi's leads were meticulous, painstakingly slow and steady. He plugged tirelessly on, deluging me with showers of ice as his ax carved each step. When he ran out the hundred feet of rope he jammed his ax into the snow to belay me. I turned my oxygen on to "2" and moved up as fast as I could, hoping to save a few moments of critical time. By the time I joined him I was completely winded, gasping for air, and sorely puzzled about why. Only late in the afternoon, when my first oxygen bottle was still going strong, did I realize what a low flow of gas my regulator was actually delivering.

Up the tongue of snow we climbed, squeezing through a passage where the walls of the Yellow Band closed in, narrowing the Couloir to shoulder width.

In four hours we had climbed only four hundred feet. It was 11 A.M. A rotten bit of vertical wall forced us to the right onto the open face. To regain the Couloir it would be necessary to climb this sixty-foot cliff, composed of two pitches split by a broken snow-covered step.

"You like to lead this one?" Willi asked.

With my oxygen off I failed to think before I replied, "Sure, I'll try it."

The rock sloped malevolently outward like shingles on a roof —rotten shingles. The covering of snow was no better than the rock. It would pretend to hold for a moment, then suddenly shatter and peel, cascading down on Willi. He sank a piton into the base of the step to anchor his belay.

I started up around the corner to the left, crampon points grating on rusty limestone. Then it became a snowplowing procedure as I searched for some sort of purchase beneath. The pick of my ax found a crack. Using the shaft for gentle leverage, I moved carefully onto the broken strata of the step. I went left again, loose debris rolling under my crampons, to the base of the final vertical rise, about eight feet high. For all its steepness, this bit was a singularly poor plastering job, nothing but wobbly rubble. I searched about for a crack, unclipped a big angle piton from my sling, and whomped it in with the hammer. It sank smoothly, as if penetrating soft butter. A gentle lift easily extracted it.

"Hmmm. Not too good," I mumbled through my mask. On the fourth try the piton gripped a bit more solidly. Deciding not to loosen it by testing, I turned to the final wall. Its steepness threw my weight out from the rock, and my pack became a downright hindrance. There was an unlimited selection of handholds, mostly portable. I shed my mittens. For a few seconds the rock felt comfortably reassuring, but cold. Then not cold any more. My eyes tried to direct sensationless fingers. Flakes peeled out beneath my crampons. I leaned out from the rock to move upward, panting like a steam engine. Damn it, it'll go; I know it will, T, I thought. But my grip was gone. I hadn't thought to turn my oxygen up.

"No soap," I called down. "Can't make it now. Too pooped."

"Come on down. There may be a way to the right."

I descended, half rappeling from the piton, which held. I had spent the better part of an hour up there. A hundred feet out we looked back. Clearly we had been on the right route, for above that last little step the gully opened out. A hundred feet higher the Yellow Band met the gray of the summit limestone. It had to get easier.

"You'd better take it," Willi. "I've wasted enough time already."

"Hell, if you couldn't make it, I'm not going to be able to do any better."

"Yes you will. It's really not that hard. I was just worn out from putting that piton in. Turn your regulator clear open, though."

Willi headed up around the corner, moving well. In ten minutes his rope was snapped through the high piton. Discarding a few unsavory holds, he gripped the rotten edge with his unmittened hands. He leaned out for the final move. His pack pulled. Crampons scraped, loosing a shower of rock from beneath his feet. He was over. He leaned against the rock, fighting for breath.

"Man, that's work. But it looks better above."

Belayed, I followed, retrieved the first piton, moved up, and went to work on the second. It wouldn't come. "Guess it's better than I thought," I shouted. "I'm going to leave it." I turned my oxygen to four liters, leaned out from the wall, and scrambled up. The extra oxygen helped, but it was surprising how breathless such a brief effort left me.

"Good lead," I panted. "That wasn't easy."

"Thanks. Let's roll."

Another rope length and we stopped. After six hours of hiss Willi's first bottle was empty. There was still a long way to go, but at least he could travel ten pounds lighter without the extra cylinder. Our altimeter read 27,900. We called Base on the walkie-talkie.

Willi: West Ridge to Base. West Ridge to Base. Over.

Base (Jim Whittaker, excitedly): This is Base here, Willi. How are you? How are things going? What's the word up there? Over.

Willi: Man, this is a real bearcat! We are nearing the top of the Yellow Band and it's mighty tough. It's too damned tough to try to go back. It would be too dangerous.

Base (Jim): I'm sure you're considering all about your exits. Why don't you leave yourself an opening? If it's not going to pan out, you can always start working your way down. I think there is always a way to come back.

Willi: Roger, Jim. We're counting on a further consultation in about two or three hundred feet. It should ease up by then! Goddammit, if we can't start moving together, we'll have to move back down. But it should be easier once the Yellow Band is passed. Over.

Base (Jim): Don't work yourself up into a bottleneck, Willi. How about rappelling? Is that possible, or don't you have any *reepschnur* or anything? Over.

Willi: There are no rappel points, Jim, absolutely no rappel points. There's nothing to secure a rope to. So it's up and over for us today . . .

While the import of his words settled upon those listening 10,000 feet below, Willi went right on:

Willi (continuing): . . . and we'll probably be getting in pretty late, maybe as late as seven or eight o'clock tonight.

As Willi talked, I looked at the mountain above. The slopes looked reasonable, as far as I could see, which wasn't very far. We sat at the base of a big, wide-open amphitheater. It looked like summits all over the place. I looked down. Descent was totally unappetizing. The rotten rock, the softening snow, the absence of even tolerable piton cracks only added to our desire to go on. Too much labor, too many sleepless nights, and too many dreams had been invested to bring us this far. We couldn't come back for another try next weekend. To go down now, even if we could have, would be descending to a future marked by one huge question: what might have been? It would not be a matter of living with our fellow man, but simply living with ourselves, with the knowledge that we had had more to give.

I listened, only mildly absorbed in Willi's conversation with Base, and looked past him at the convexity of rock cutting off our view of the gully we had ascended. Above—a snowfield, gray walls, then blue-black sky. We were committed. An invisible barrier sliced through the mountain beneath our feet, cutting us off from the world below. Though we could see through, all we saw was infinitely remote. The ethereal link provided by our radio only intensified our separation. My wife and children seemed suddenly close. Yet home, life itself, lay only over the top of Everest and down the other side. Suppose

we fail? The thought brought no remorse, no fear. Once entertained, it hardly seemed even interesting. What now mattered most was right here: Willi and I, tied together on a rope, and the mountain, its summit not inaccessibly far above. The reason we had come was within our grasp. We belonged to the mountain and it to us. There was anxiety, to be sure, but it was all but lost in a feeling of calm, of pleasure at the joy of climbing. That we couldn't go down only made easier that which we really wanted to do. That we might not get there was scarcely conceivable.

Willi was still talking.

Willi: Any news of Barry and Lute? Over.

Jim: I haven't heard a word from them. Over.

Willi: How about Dingman?

Jim: No word from Dingman. We've heard nothing, nothing at all.

Willi: Well listen, if you do get hold of Dingman, tell him to put a light in the window because we're headed for the summit, Jim. We can't possibly get back to our camp now. Over.

I stuffed the radio back in Willi's pack. It was 1 P.M. From here we could both climb at the same time, moving across the last of the yellow slabs. Another hundred feet and the Yellow Band was below us. A steep tongue of snow flared wide, penetrating the gray strata that capped the mountain. The snow was hard, almost ice-hard in places. We had only to bend our ankles, firmly plant all twelve crampon points, and walk uphill. At last, we were moving, though it would have appeared painfully slow to a distant bystander.

As we climbed out of the Couloir the pieces of the puzzle fell into place. That snow rib ahead on the left skyline should lead us to the Summit Snowfield, a patch of perpetual white clinging to the North Face at the base of Everest's final pyramid. By three we were on the Snowfield. We had been climbing for eight hours and knew we needed to take time to refuel. At a shaly outcrop of rock we stopped for lunch. There was a decision to be made. We could either cut straight up the northeast ridge and follow it west to the summit, or we could traverse the face and regain the West Ridge. From where we sat, the Ridge looked easier. Besides, it was the route we'd intended in the first place.

We split a quart of lemonade that was slushy with ice. In spite of its down parka wrapping, the other bottle was already frozen solid, as were the kippered snacks. They were almost tasteless but we downed them more with dutiful thoughts of calories than with pleasure.

To save time we moved together, diagonaling upward across down-sloping slabs of rotten shale. There were no possible stances from which to belay each other. Then snow again, and Willi kicked steps, fastidiously picking a route between the outcropping rocks. Though still carting my full load of oxygen bottles, I was beginning to feel quite strong. With this excess energy came impatience, and an unconscious anxiety over the high stakes for which we were playing and the lateness of the day. Why the hell is Willi going so damned slow? I thought. And a little later: He should cut over to the Ridge now; it'll be a lot easier.

I shouted into the wind, "Hold up, Willi!" He pretended not to hear me as he started up the rock. It seemed terribly important to tell him to go to the right. I tugged on the rope. "Damn it, wait up, Willi!" Stopped by a taut rope and an unyielding Hornbein, he turned, and with some irritation anchored his ax while I hastened to join him. He was perched, through no choice of his own, in rather cramped, precarious quarters. I sheepishly apologized.

We were on rock now. One rope length, crampons scraping, brought us to the crest of the West Ridge for the first time since we'd left camp 4W yesterday morning. The South Face fell eight thousand feet to the tiny tents of Advance Base. Lhotse, straight across the face, was below us now. And near at hand, a hundred and fifty feet higher, the South Summit of Everest shone in the afternoon sun. We were within four hundred feet of the top! The wind whipped across the ridge from the north at nearly sixty miles an hour. Far below, peak shadows reached long across the cloud-filled valleys. Above, the Ridge rose, a twisting, rocky spine.

We shed crampons and overboots to tackle this next rocky bit with the comforting grip of cleated rubber soles. Here I unloaded my first oxygen bottle though it was not quite empty. It had lasted ten hours, which obviously meant I'd be getting a lower flow than indicated by the regulator. Resisting Willi's suggestion to drop the cylinder off the South Face, I left it for some unknown posterity. When I resaddled ten pounds lighter, I felt I could float to the top.

The rock was firm, at least in comparison with our fare thus far. Climbing one at a time, we experienced the joy of delicate moves on tiny holds. The going was a wonderful pleasure, almost like a day in the Rockies. With the sheer drop to the Cwm beneath us, we measured off another four rope lengths. Solid rock gave way to crud, then snow. A thin, firm, knife-edge of white pointed gently toward the sky. Buffeted by the wind, we laced our crampons on, racing each other with rapidly numbing fingers. It took nearly twenty minutes. Then we were off again, squandering oxygen at three liters per minute since time seemed the shorter commodity at the moment. We moved together, Willi in front. It seemed almost as if we were cheating, using oxygen; we could nearly run this final bit.

Ahead the North and South ridges converged to a point. Surely the summit wasn't that near? It must be off behind. Willi stopped. What's he waiting for, I wondered as I moved to join him. With a feeling of disbelief I looked up. Forty feet ahead tattered and whipped by the wind was the flag Jim had left three weeks before. It was 6:15. The sun's rays sheered horizontally across the summit. We hugged each other as tears welled up, ran down across our oxygen masks, and turned to ice.

I believe that no man can be completely able to summon all his strength, all his will, all his energy, for the last desperate move, till he is convinced the last bridge is down behind him and that there is nowhere to go but on.   —HEINRICH HARRER

15. . . . and Miles to Go . . .

JUST ROCK, a dome of snow, the deep blue sky, and a hunk of orange-painted metal from which a shredded American flag cracked in the wind. Nothing more. Except two tiny figures walking together those last few feet to the top of the earth.

For twenty minutes we stayed there. The last brilliance of the day cast the shadow of our summit on the cloud plain a hundred miles to the east. Valleys were filled with the indistinct purple haze of evening, concealing the dwellings of man we knew were there. The chill roar of wind made speaking difficult, heightening our feeling of remoteness. The flag left there seemed a feeble gesture of man that had no purpose but to accentuate the isolation. The two of us who had dreamed months before of sharing this moment were linked by a thin line of rope, joined in the intensity of companionship to those inaccessibly far below, Al and Barry and Dick—and Jake.

From a pitch of intense emotional and physical drive it was only partly possible to become suddenly, completely the philosopher of a balmy afternoon. The head of steam was too great, and the demands on it still remained. We have a long way to go to get down, I thought. But the prospect of descent of an unknown side of the mountain in the dark caused me less anxiety than many other occasions had. I had a blind, fatalistic faith that, having succeeded in coming this far, we could not fail to get down. The moment became an end in itself.

There were many things savored in this brief time. Even with our oxygen turned off we had no problem performing those summit obeisances, photographing the fading day (it's a wonderful place to be for sunset photographs), smiling behind our masks for the inevitable "I was there" picture. Willi wrapped the kata given him by Ang Dorje about the flag pole and planted Andy Bakewell's crucifix alongside it in the snow; Lhotse and Makalu, below us, were a contrast of sun-blazed snow etched against the darkness of evening shadow. We felt the lonely beauty of the evening, the immense roaring silence of the wind, the tenuousness of our tie to all below. There was a hint of fear, not for our lives, but of a vast unknown which pressed in upon us. A fleeting feeling of disappointment— that after all those dreams and questions this was only a mountaintop—gave way to the suspicion that maybe there was something more, something beyond the three-dimensional form of the moment. If only it could be perceived.

But it was late. The memories had to be stored, the meanings taken down. The question of why we had come was not now to be answered, yet something up here must yield an answer, something only dimly felt, comprehended by senses reaching farther yet than the point on which we stood; reaching for understanding, which hovered but a few steps higher. The answers lay not on the summit of Everest, nor in the sky above it, but in the world to which we belonged and must now return.

Footprints in the snow told that Lute and Barrel had been here. We'd have a path to follow as long as light remained.

"Want to go first?" Willi asked. He began to coil the rope.

Looking down the corniced edge, I thought of the added protection of a rope from above. "Doesn't matter, Willi. Either way."

O.K. Why don't I go first then?" he said, handing me the coil. Paying out the rope as he disappeared below me I wondered, Is Unsoeld tired? It was hard to believe. Still he'd worked hard; he had a right to be weary. Starting sluggishly, I'd felt stronger as we climbed. So now we would reverse roles. Going up had been pretty much Willi's show; going down would be mine. I dropped the last coil and started after him.

Fifty feet from the top we stopped at a patch of exposed rock. Only the summit of Everest, shining pink, remained above the shadow sea. Willi radioed to Maynard Miller at Advance Base that we were headed for the South Col. It was 6:35 P.M.

We almost ran along the crest, trusting Lute and Barrel's track to keep us a safe distance from the cornice edge. Have to reach the South Summit before dark, I thought, or we'll never find the way. The sun dropped below the jagged horizon. We didn't need goggles any more. There was a loud hiss as I banged my oxygen bottle against the ice wall. Damn! Something's broken. I reached back and turned off the valve. Without oxygen, I tried to keep pace with the rope disappearing over the edge ahead. Vision dimmed, the ground began to move. I stopped till things cleared, waved my arms and shouted into the wind for Willi to hold up. The taut rope finally stopped him. I tightened the regulator, then turned the oxygen on. No hiss! To my relief it had only been jarred loose. On oxygen again, I could move rapidly. Up twenty feet, and we were on the South Summit. It was 7:15.

Thank God for the footprints. Without them, we'd have had a tough time deciding which way to go. We hurried on, facing outward, driving our heels into the steep snow. By 7:30 it was dark. We took out the flashlight and resumed the descent. The batteries, dregs of the Expedition, had not been helped by our session with Emerson's diary the night before; they quickly faded. There was pitiful humor as Willi probed, holding the light a few inches off the snow to catch some sign of tracks. You could order your eyes to see, but nothing in the blackness complied.

We moved slowly now. Willi was only a voice and an occasional faint flicker of light to point the way. No fear, no worry, no strangeness, just complete absorption. The drive which had carried us to a nebulous goal was replaced by simple desire for survival. There was no time to dwell on the uniqueness of our situation. We climbed carefully, from years of habit. At a rock outcrop we paused. Which way? Willi groped to the right along a corniced edge. In my imagination, I filled in the void.

"No tracks over here," Willi called.

"Maybe we should dig in here for the night."

"I don't know. Dave and Girmi should be at 6."

We shouted into the night, and the wind engulfed our call. A lull. Again we shouted. "Helloooo," the wind answered. Or was it the wind?

"Hellooo," we called once more.

"Helloo," came back faintly. That wasn't the wind!

"To the left, Willi."

"O.K., go ahead."

In the blackness I couldn't see my feet. Each foot groped cautiously, feeling its way down, trusting to the pattern set by its predecessor. Slowly left, right, left, crampons biting into the snow, right, left, . . .

"*Willeeee!*" I yelled as I somersaulted into space. The rope came taut, and with a soft thud I landed.

"Seems to be a cornice there," I called from beneath the wall. "I'll belay you from here."

Willi sleepwalked down to the edge. The dim outline of his foot wavered until it met my guiding hand. His arrival lacked the flair of my descent. It was well that the one of lighter weight had gone first.

Gusts buffeted from all directions, threatening to dislodge us from the slope. Above a cliff we paused, untied, cut the rope in half, and tied in again. It didn't help; even five feet behind I couldn't see Willi. Sometimes the snow was good, sometimes it was soft, sometimes it lay shallow over rocks so we could only drive our axes in an inch or two. With these psychological belays, we wandered slowly down, closer to the answering shouts. The wind was dying, and so was the flashlight, now no more than an orange glow illuminating nothing. The stars, brilliant above, cast no light on the snow. Willi's oxygen ran out. He slowed, suddenly feeling much wearier.

The voices were close now. Were they coming from those two black shapes on the snow? Or were those rocks?

"Shine your light down here," a voice called.

"Where? Shine yours up here," I answered.

"Don't have one," came the reply.

Then we were with them—not Dave and Girmi, but Lute and Barrel. They were near exhaustion, shivering lumps curled on the snow. Barrel in particular was far gone. Anxious hungering for air through the previous night, and the near catastrophe when their tent caught fire in the morning, had left him tired before they even started. Determination got him to the top, but now he no longer cared. He only wanted to be left alone. Lute was also tired. Because of Barrel's condition he'd had to bear the brunt of the climbing labor. His eyes were painfully burned, perhaps by the fire, perhaps by the sun and wind. From sheer fatigue they had stopped thinking. Their oxygen was gone, except for a bit Lute had saved for Barrel; but they were too weak to make the change.

At 9:30 we were still a thousand feet above Camp 6. Willi sat down on the snow, and I walked over to get Lute's oxygen for Barrel. As I unscrewed Lute's regulator from the bottle, he explained why they were still there. Because of the stove fire that had sent them diving from the tent, they were an hour late in starting. It was 3:30 P.M. when they reached the summit. Seeing no sign of movement down the west side,

they figured no one would be any later than they were. At 4:15 they started down. Fatigue slowed their descent. Just after dark they had stopped to rest and were preparing to move when they heard shouts. Dave and Girmi, they thought. No —the sounds seemed to be coming from above. Willi and Tom! So they waited, shivering.

I removed Barrel's regulator from his empty bottle and screwed it into Lute's. We were together now, sharing the support so vigorously debated a week before. Lute would know the way back to their camp, even in the dark. All we had to do was help them down. Fumbling with unfeeling fingers, I tried to attach Barrel's oxygen hose to the regulator. Damn! Can't make the connection. My fingers scraped uncoördinately against the cold metal. Try again. There it goes. Then, quickly, numb fingers clumsy, back into mittens. Feeling slowly returned, and pain. Then, the pain went and the fingers were warm again.

Willi remembered the Dexedrine I had dropped into my shirt pocket the evening before. I fished out two pills—one for Barrel and one for Lute. Barrel was better with oxygen, but why I had balked at his communal use of Lute's regulator, I cannot say. Lack of oxygen? Fatigue? It was fifteen hours since we'd started our climb. Or was it that my thoughts were too busy with another problem? We had to keep moving or freeze.

I led off. Lute followed in my footsteps to point out the route. Lost in the darkness sixty feet back on our ropes, Willi and Barrel followed. The track was more sensed than seen, but it was easier now, not so steep. My eyes watered from searching for the black holes punched in the snow by Lute's and Barrel's axes during their ascent. We walked to the left of the crest, three feet down, ramming our axes into the narrow edge. Thirty feet, and the rope came taut as Barrel collapsed in the snow, bringing the entire caravan to a halt. Lute sat down behind me. Got to keep moving. We'll never get there.

We had almost no contact with the back of the line. When the rope came taut, we stopped, when it loosened we moved on. Somewhere my oxygen ran out, but we were going too slow for me to notice the difference. Ought to dump the empty bottle, I thought, but it was too much trouble to take off my pack.

Heat lightning flashed along the plains to the east, too distant to light our way. Rocks that showed in the snow below seemed to get no closer as the hours passed. Follow the ax holes. Where'd they go? Not sure. There's another.

"Now where, Lute?"

"Can't see, Tom." Lute said. "Can't see a damn thing. We've got to turn down a gully between some rocks."

"Which gully. There's two or three."

"Don't know, Tom."

"Think, Lute. Try to remember. We've got to get to 6."

"I don't know. I just can't see."

Again and again I questioned, badgering, trying to extract some hint. But half blind and weary, Lute had no answer. We plodded on. The rocks came slowly closer.

Once the rope jerked tight, nearly pulling me off balance. Damn! What's going on? I turned and looked at Lute's dim form lying on the snow a few feet further down the Kangshung Face. His fall had been effectively if uncomfortably arrested when his neck snagged the rope between Willi and me.

We turned off the crest, toward the rocks. Tongues of snow pierced the cliffs below. But which one? It was too dangerous to plunge on. After midnight we reached the rocks. It had taken nearly three hours to descend four hundred feet, maybe fifteen minutes' worth by daylight.

Tired. No hope of finding camp in the darkness. No choice but to wait for day. Packs off. Willi and I slipped into our down parkas. In the dark, numb fingers couldn't start the zippers. We settled to the ground, curled as small as possible atop our pack frames. Lute and Barry were somewhere behind, apart, each alone. Willi and I tried hugging each other to salvage warmth, but my uncontrollable shivering made it impossible.

The oxygen was gone, but the mask helped a little for warmth. Feet, cooling, began to hurt. I withdrew my hands from the warmth of my crotch and loosened crampon bindings and boot laces, but my feet stayed cold. Willi offered to rub them. We removed boots and socks and planted both my feet against his stomach. No sensation returned.

Tired by the awkward position, and frustrated by the result, we gave it up. I slid my feet back into socks and boots, but couldn't tie them. I offered to warm Willi's feet. Thinking that his freedom from pain was due to a high tolerance of cold, he declined. We were too weary to realize the reason for his comfort.

The night was overpoweringly empty. Stars shed cold unshimmering light. The heat lightning dancing along the plains spoke of a world of warmth and flatness. The black silhouette of Lhotse lurked half sensed, half seen, still below. Only the ridge on which we were rose higher, disappearing into the night, a last lonely outpost of the world.

Mostly there was nothing. We hung suspended in a timeless void. The wind died, and there was silence. Even without wind it was cold. I could reach back and touch Lute or Barrel lying head to toe above me. They seemed miles away.

Unsignaled, unembellished, the hours passed. Intense cold penetrated, carrying with it the realization that each of us was completely alone. Nothing Willi could do for me or I for him. No team now, just each of us, imprisoned with his own discomfort, his own thoughts, his own will to survive.

Yet for me, survival was hardly a conscious thought. Nothing to plan, nothing to push for, nothing to do but shiver and wait for the sun to rise. I floated in a dreamlike eternity, devoid of plans, fears, regrets. The heat lightning, Lhotse, my companions, discomfort, all were there—yet not there. Death had no meaning, nor, for that matter, did life. Survival was no concern, no issue. Only a dulled impatience for the sun to rise tied my formless thoughts to the future.

About 4:00 the sky began to lighten along the eastern rim, baring the bulk of Kangchenjunga. The sun was slow in following, interminably slow. Not till after 5:00 did it finally come, its light streaming through the South Col, blazing yellow across the Nuptse Wall, then onto the white wave crest of peaks far below. We watched as if our own life was being born again. Then as the cold yellow light touched us, we rose. There were still miles to go.

Play for more than you can afford to lose, and you will learn the game.
—CHURCHILL

Now understand me well—It is provided in the essence of things, that from any fruition of success, no matter what, shall come forth something to make a greater struggle necessary.

—WALT WHITMAN

16. . . . Before I Sleep

THE REST is like a photograph with little depth of field, the focused moments crystal sharp against a blurred background of fatigue. We descended the gully I had been unable to find in the dark. Round the corner, Dave and Girmi were coming toward us. They thought they heard shouts in the night and had started up, but their own calls were followed only by silence. Now, as they came in search of the bodies of Lute and Barry they saw people coming down—not just two, but four. Dave puzzled a moment before he understood.

The tents at Camp 6—and we were home from the mountain. Nima Dorje brought tea. We shed boots. I stared blankly at the marble-white soles of Willi's feet. They were cold and hard as ice. We filled in Emerson's diary for the last time, then started down.

With wind tearing snow from its rocky plain, the South Col was as desolate and uninviting as it had always been described. We sought shelter in the tents at Camp 5 for lunch, then emerged into the gale. Across the Geneva Spur, out of the wind, onto the open sweep of the Lhotse Face we plodded in somber procession. Dave led gently, patiently; the four behind rocked along, feet apart to keep from falling. Only for Willi and me was this side of the mountain new. Like tourists we looked around, forgetting fatigue for the moment.

At Camp 4 we stopped to melt water, then continued with the setting sun, walking through dusk into darkness as Dave guided us among crevasses, down the Cwm. It was a mystery to me how he found the way. I walked along at the back, following the flashlight. Sometimes Willi stopped and I would nearly bump into him. We waited while Dave searched, then moved on. No one complained.

At 10:30 P.M. we arrived at Advance Base. Dick, Barry, and Al were down from the Ridge, waiting. Frozen feet and Barrel's hands were thawed in warm water. Finally to bed, after almost two days. Short a sleeping bag, Willi and I shared one as best we could.

May 24 we were late starting, tired. Lute, Willi, and Barrel walked on thawed feet. It was too dangerous to carry them down through the Icefall. Willi, ahead of me on the rope, heeled down like an awkward clown. The codeine wasn't enough to prevent cries of pain when he stubbed his toes against the snow. I cried as I walked behind, unharmed.

At Camp 1 Maynard nursed us like a mother hen, serving us water laboriously melted from ice samples drilled from the glacier for analysis. Then down through the Icefall, past Jake's grave—and a feeling of finality. It's all done. The dream's finished.

No rest. The next day, a grim gray one, we departed Base. From low-hanging clouds wet snow fell. Willi, Barrel, and Lute were loaded aboard porters to be carried down over the rocky moraine. It was easier walking.

At Gorak Shep we paused. On a huge boulder a Sherpa craftsman had patiently carved:

IN MEMORY OF JOHN E. BREITENBACH,
AMERICAN MOUNT EVEREST EXPEDITION, 1963.

Clouds concealed the mountain that was Jake's grave.

As we descended, the falling snow gave way to a fine drizzle. There was nothing to see; just one foot, then another. But slowly a change came, something that no matter how many times experienced, is always new, like life. It *was* life. From ice and snow and rock, we descended to a world of living things, of green—grass and trees and bushes. There was no taking it for granted. Spring had come, and even the gray drizzle imparted a wet sheen to all that grew. At Pheriche flowers bloomed in the meadows.

Lying in bed, Willi and I listened to a sound that wasn't identifiable, so foreign was it to the place—the chopping whir as a helicopter circled, searching for a place to light. In a flurry of activity Willi and Barrel were loaded aboard. The helicopter rose from the hilltop above the village and dipped into the distance. The chop-chop-chop of the blades faded, until finally the craft itself was lost in the massive backdrop. The departure was too unreal, too much a part of another world, to be really comprehended. Less than five days after they had stood on the summit of Everest, Barrel and Willi were back in Kathmandu. For them the Expedition was ended. Now all that remained was weeks in bed, sitting, rocking in pain, waiting for toes to mummify to the time for amputation.

Up over barren passes made forbidding by mist and a chill wind, we traveled. Hard work. Then down through forests of rain-drenched rhododendrons, blossoming pastels of pink and lavendar. Toes hurt. Two weeks to Kathmandu. Feet slipped on the muddy path. Everything was wet.

Everest is a harsh and hostile immensity. Whoever challenges it declares war. He must mount his assault with the skill and ruthlessness of a military operation. And when the battle ends, the mountain remains unvanquished. There are no true victors, only survivors.

—BARRY BISHOP

We were finished. Everest was climbed; nothing to push for now. Existence knew only the instant, counting steps, falling asleep each time we stopped to rest beside the trail. Lester, Emerson, and I talked about motivation; for me it was all gone. It was a time of relaxation, a time when senses were tuned to perceive, but nothing was left to give.

Pleasure lay half-hidden beneath discomfort, fatigue, loneliness. Willi was gone. The gap where he had been was filled with a question: Why hadn't I known that his feet were numb? Surely I could have done something, if only . . . I was too weary to know the question couldn't be resolved. Half of me seemed to have gone with him; the other half was isolated from my companions by an experience I couldn't share and by the feeling that something was ending that had come to mean too much. Talk of home, of the first evening in the Yak and Yeti Bar, of the reception that waited, was it really so important? Did it warrant the rush?

We'd climbed Everest. What good was it to Jake? To Willi, to Barrel? To Norman, with Everest all done now? And to the rest of us? What waits? What price less tangible than toes? There must be something more to it than toiling over the top of another, albeit expensive, mountain. Perhaps there was something of the nobility-that-is-man in it somewhere, but it was hard to be sure.

Yes, it satisfied in a way. Not just climbing the mountain, but the entire effort—the creating something, the few of us molding it from the beginning. With a lot of luck we'd succeeded. But what had we proved?

Existence on a mountain is simple. Seldom in life does it come any simpler: survival, plus the striving toward a summit.

The goal is solidly, three-dimensionally there—you can see it, touch it, stand upon it—the way to reach it well defined, the energy of all directed toward its achievement. It is this simplicity that strips the veneer off civilization and makes that which is meaningful easier to come by—the pleasure of deep companionship, moments of uninhibited humor, the tasting of hardship, sorrow, beauty, joy. But it is this very simplicity that may prevent finding answers to the questions I had asked as we approached the mountain.

Then I had been unsure that I could survive and function in a world so foreign to my normal existence. Now I felt at home here, no longer overly afraid. Each step toward Kathmandu carried me back toward the known, yet toward many things terribly unknown, toward goals unclear, to be reached by paths undefined.

Beneath fatigue lurked the suspicion that the answers I sought were not to be found on a mountain. What possible difference could climbing Everest make? Certainly the mountain hadn't been changed. Even now wind and falling snow would have obliterated most signs of our having been there. Was I any greater for having stood on the highest place on earth? Within the wasted figure that stumbled weary and fearful back toward home there was no question about the answer to that one.

It had been a wonderful dream, but now all that lingered was the memory. The dream was ended.

Everest must join the realities of my existence, commonplace and otherwise. The goal, unattainable, had been attained. Or had it? The questions, many of them, remained. And the answers? It is strange how when a dream is fulfilled there is little left but doubt.

Never let success hide its emptiness from you, achievement its nothingness, toil its desolation. And so keep alive the incentive to push on further, that pain in the soul which drives us beyond ourselves.
Whither? That I don't know. That I don't ask to know.

—DAG HAMMARSKJOLD

JOHN EDGAR BREITENBACH
1935-1963

John Edgar Breitenbach was killed on March 23, 1963, in the Khumbu Icefall of Mount Everest by a collapsing wall of ice.

Jake climbed throughout North America, made significant ascents in the Tetons, climbed McKinley by the West Buttress and again by the western rim of the South Face, and attempted Mount Steele in the St. Elias Range. He was a member of the 1963 American Mount Everest Expedition. Jake was a fine mountaineer. He never climbed Mount Owen, although he went to within a yard of the summit many times. He thought that someday he might want to climb Owen for the first time, and perhaps he enjoyed the courting.

He graduated in mathematics from Oregon State College, then made his home in Jackson Hole, Wyoming, where he guided for six years and operated a ski shop. He is survived by his wife, his parents, a brother, and his friends, all of whom loved him.

Exultant, tolerant of himself and others, delighted by new horizons, Jake was always searching, searching harder than most. He also lived harder than most and was once a swinger of birches. He liked sunsets, the New World Symphony, yellow rock in the sunlight, watching his own history, cold nights, catching a fish. He was very happy in the icefall the day he died, though he knew that mountains sometimes move.

Most of all, Jake scribed the future through his friends, which imprint will survive. His friends will recognize the epitaph Jake always wanted—Long live the Crow.

—JAMES BARRY CORBET

. . . The sun still rises in the east, and for nearly two centuries now mountaineers have been setting out to meet him each summer's day, after consulting the stars and the cold. . . .

Grey limestone or ruddy granite, ice of the gully or the serac, blown snow or snowy cornice, smell of rock, scent of flowers, delicate saxifrage or sub-Himalayan forest, starlight or storms, sun-scorched terrace, unreal frontiers, friendship between two beings for better or for worse—to these do we belong.

—GASTON REBUFFAT

Only those who have throughout long years nourished a great, almost an intemperate, desire, and have then seen it realised exactly as they most wished, can understand the feeling of profound gratitude and satisfaction which filled our hearts on the descent. It was not pride of conquest. It was rather the sentiment of communion, granted as a privilege, with the high places of the earth; the sentiment that we had been permitted not only to lift up covetous eyes unto these hills, secret and lonely since the beginning of the world, but to come at them hardily, to take a place in the hitherto sealed-up intimacy of their retreats, to be alive there, and from their heights to look on all things as from the windows of the sky.

—HUDSON STUCK, 1913
quoted by Gaston Rebuffat

Mountain Prospect

PHOTOGRAPHS BY NORMAN G. DYHRENFURTH

To sit on rocks, to muse o'er flood and fell,
To slowly trace the forest's shady scene,
Where things that own not man's dominion dwell,
And mortal foot hath ne'er, or rarely been;
To climb the trackless mountain all unseen,

This is not solitude, 'tis but to hold
converse with nature's charms, and
   see her stores unrolled.

—BYRON

Eastward the . . . downs rose, ridge behind ridge into the morning, and vanished out of
eyesight into a guess; it was no more than a guess of blue and a remote white glimmer
blending with the hem of the sky, but it spoke to them, out of memory and old tales,
of the high and distant mountains.

—J. R. R. TOLKIEN

Makalu (left) from near Dhankuta

The mountains are the oldest descendants of the creator god, Prajapati. They had wings, with which they flew about, alighting where it pleased them. Indra cut off their wings and made fast the earth with the mountains. The wings which had been cut off became storm clouds, which is why they float above the mountains, for that is where they belonged.

—TONI HAGEN

Fields near Panchkal

When we begin to notice how shy Nature is of company we are beginning to know a little about the natural world to which we belong. In any world which belongs to civilized humanity, in a crowd of town or school, Nature is moody if present at all, and she can behave as outrageously as Caliban. In the open air, if mortals seek her with their human cross-purposes still uppermost in mind, if they "hunt her in couples," she will appear to envelop them with superficial sympathy, but elude them all the while with the secret midleading of a Puck. Only to those who walk alone by wood or sea or hill does she appear as Ariel, a sprite and fitful still, but a sprite in their occasional service; ready even at times to act as an interpreter of her own enchantments if the service they ask for is to be shown, behind the magic of form and colour, something of the principles of order and slower change that govern natural existences not made in man's image. . . . in these places, at these times, if we are alone, we may become aware of personalities in landscape and sound and motion as vivacious as our own but not humanly definable, and of new qualities of emotion manifested in them which burst through the poor wrappings of names which give to them, anger or heartbreak or laughter, as through tatters of wet tissue-paper.

—GOEFFREY WINTHROP YOUNG

The demagogues . . . who have already caused the death of several civilizations, harass men so that they will not reflect; manage to keep them herded together in crowds so that they cannot reconstruct their individuality in the one place where it can be reconstructed, which is in solitude.

—ORTEGA Y GASSET

Pool near Dhankuta

One of the misfortunes of advancing age is that you get out of touch with the sunrise. You take it for granted, and it is over and done with before you settle yourself for the daily routine. That is one reason, I think, why, when we grow older, the days seem shorter. We miss the high moments of their beginning.

—JOHN BUCHAN
(*Lord Tweedsmuir*)

Boy and swing near Chaubas

. . . But give me a man at least moderately endowed in mind and body, educated liberally, and not too much given to idleness and luxury or to lust; also I should wish him curious about natural objects and an admirer of them, so that even from the contemplation and admiration of the mighty works of the Supreme Architect & of the enormour variety of nature as it exhibits itself in the mountains, as though in a single vast pile, the delight of his spirit might be added to the harmonious delight of all his senses; what other sort of pleasure will you find, pray, at least within the bounds of nature, more honorable, more complete, and more perfect from every point of view? But walking itself and fatigue are tiresome and tedious. There is also danger in the difficulties of the region and in the steep places. The allurements of food and bed are lacking. Grant that these things are true; it will be pleasant thereafter to recall the toils and the dangers; it will gratify you to turn over these things in your mind and to tell them to friends.

—CONRAD GESNER (1555)

En route to the Solo Khumbu, base of Chumlung in distance

In his laborious efforts to attain mountain tops where the air is lighter and purer, the climber gains new strength of limb. In the endeavour to overcome obstacles of the way, the soul trains itself to conquer difficulties; and the Spectacle of the vast horizon, which from the highest crest offers itself on all sides to the eyes, raises his spirit to the Divine Author and Sovereign of Natures.

—POPE PIUS XI

And always, in joyous bivouacs as in sad ones, in those which preceded victory as in those which followed defeat, there was always the same fascination that I now experienced once more—a secret thrill, a sense of wonder, an expectation of something indefinable, something mysterious, that was about to become manifest.

Now that the agony of my long and sustained effort had ceased, I began to hear a confused murmur of voices and of sounds that came from every side, rising from the valley and falling from the summit; starting from afar, it increased in intensity as it drew nearer, and then rolled swiftly away in the distance. It was like the sighs of spirits flying above my head. Amid the low yet powerful sounds of the huge chorus I could sometimes distinguish a sharper note, as of anger or lamentation, which soon ceased, while another voice was uplifted in answer from afar.

This was the high dialogue between the mountains and the sky, but on that night all the voices, great and small, seemed to seek out the tiny mortal who lay lonely and abandoned on the mountain's bosom, and to relate to him a long and wonderful tale, ancient as the world itself.

I was shivering with a strange mixture of curiosity and fear. The influence of the hour and the place awoke in me a latent primeval terror, an unsuspected legacy from ancient tribes that had lived without hearth or roof. My quivering nerves were subject to the same gloomy influences as had swayed my mysterious far-off ancestors, who witnessed the terrible anger of the glaciers on this earth. Then all fell silent once more. With the dropping of the evening breeze and the fading of the last glow, the mountains seemed to die; the fair light was gone, the light which alone lends life and movement to the rocks, which gives variation to their outlines and their hues, which creates shadows in the couloirs and fire on the summits, which softens or hardens the expressions of the mountain's face, accentuates its wrinkles or smooths its brow.

By night a mountain's mighty limbs are as still as if they were frozen to death, and its gigantic face stiffens into an immutable expression of mystery. We were fated to spend a whole night in the arms of the immense corpse, and I instinctively pressed my arms against my breast, that I might feel the warmth of my own body and protect it from freezing in that embrace of stone.

I sought to begin a conversation with my friends, in my desire to hear a human voice once more, but the talk soon flagged: we had nothing to tell each other.

—GUIDO REY (c. 1900)

Even if this noble peak were to be the last milestone on my journey, even if the hour had struck when I must part from the sweet illusions that have nourished my best years, if I had now plucked the last fruit of a passion that dated from the day when my spirit first tasted the virile enjoyments of life, yet I ought still to have rejoiced that I had answered once more with enthusiasm to the wild call of my mountains, and to have left them, not sated, but satisfied with the vigour they had given me, to have saluted them with gratitude in that they alone had allowed me to approach visions which would not have been vouchsafed to me otherwise. . . .

That which once appeared as simply an amusement for my idle hours and an outlet for the superabundant energy of youth, has now become a strict element in the regulation of my life and a necessary support for my declining strength; in my heart, which is now closed to the ingenuous conceits of my early years, insensible to the rivalries which incited me of yore to deeds of daring, careless of the applause which it formerly prized as the guerdon of victory, there is now but one pure flame, that burns gently and steadily, and does not flicker with the breath of praise or blame. I know that were I to return to the place whence I started, I should again choose without hesitation the road to the mountains.

But life's span is short; the fatal year is close at hand when the approach of the summer will no longer be a signal for the secret and anxious consideration of bold and cherished plans, for preparations hidden from all, and for the usual departure towards the unknown. Rope and sack and axe will remain hanging on the wall like trophies of ancient arms. I shall no longer return from my mysterious absences with garments torn and hands peeled, nor shall I come proudly home with my face all burned by the Alpine sun. . . .

And from the sparkling slopes, from the immense fields of snow, from the pure white peaks, the memories of past hours will descend to me in slow procession, and each one will awaken an interest in me, and will look upon me with a familiar glance and tell me its name. . . .

Some go past me mysteriously and gravely, as if they bore a secret grief; these are the memories of the silent hours of defeat, and they seem hardly to refrain from weeping, not knowing that I loved them more than the others, that I would give ten victories for each of them. . . .

There follow the memories of the maturer hours, more recent ones, which will smile to me, but I read on their sunburnt faces the expression and the furrows of experience, and a more austere and calmer joy; these are the dizzy hours of my latest expeditions . . . but their breathless voices die away in the infinite mystery of the mountains. And all they are able to tell is little naïve tales of their life of everlasting youth, and simple words

whispered in the stress of danger, or songs sung loudly in chorus in the peaceful valleys; tales of hasty frugal meals taken on lofty ridges between two precipices, or of sweet rests in quiet huts by the light of a tiny lantern; of swinging ropes and broken axes, of brave young comrades and of old friends that are gone.

They have drunk at many a cold spring, been buffeted by all the winds, felt the weight of the sack and the jerks of the rope, known the wounds of piercing frost and of sharp pointed rocks. . . .

Perhaps amongst the visions of my old age there will come at times to my weary mind a mysterious image, full of power and sweetness, composed of all the peaks I have known, and I shall anxiously seek to trace and to recognize one by one the charming features that were once so familiar to me, though they are now confused and intermingled amid the mists of dreams and time; and I shall joyfully see the pure, grim outline of my last love leap forth by the side of the smiling face of my first.

But it grew cold on the mountain; the sky had sunk till it touched the summit of the Pala; the darkness accentuated the deep melancholy of its cliffs, which need the smile of the sun. The clouds were thickening all round, but here and there they were torn asunder by sharp points, like the fingers of a great fleshless hand, phantom peaks that came and went in the shadow. . . .

. . . It seemed as if the sun were extinguished for ever and the whole world submerged, and as if nothing survived the deluge but the tiny crag on which we were assembled, huddled close together, benumbed, with our hands in our pockets and our collars turned up; we might have been the last living creatures on earth, gnawing the last piece of bread, under the shelter of a heap of stones which stood as a monument to a bygone hour of human triumph; the sleet whirled about us, but we tiny mortals with chattering teeth felt a glow in our hearts, and we cheerfully bared our burning faces to the fury of the wind; lost amid the solitude, we peopled it with our thoughts and discovered a blaze of glory in the dark mists; our souls were illuminated by a divine vision of purity and beauty.

Our journey was done. Very soon we should leave this rock on which for a short hour we had known freedom and power; returning to the plain, we should find there the humble realities of life once more.

Why, then, should we hurry to descend?

Should we ever again know such moments of peace? Ever again be together, my friend and I, on the roof of the world?

I said . . . : "Let us stop here a little while longer! It is good to rest on the summit, and to dream amongst the clouds for a few short moments in one's life."

—GUIDO REY (c. 1912)

But if adventure has a final and all-embracing motive it is surely this: we go out because it is in our nature to go out, to climb the mountains and sail the seas, to fly to the planets and plunge into the depths of the oceans. By doing these things we make touch with something outside or behind, which strangely seems to approve our doing them. We extend our horizon, we expand our being, we revel in a mastery of ourselves which gives an impression, mainly illusory, that we are masters of our world. In a word, we are men, and when man ceases to do these things, he is no longer man.

—WILFRED NOYCE

Honga Basin peaks and Ama Dablan from near Pheriche

The stone grows old.
Eternity is not for stones.
But I shall go down from this airy space, this swift white
    peace, this stinging exultation;
And time will close about me, and my soul stir to the
    rhythm of the daily round.
Yet, having known, life will not press so close,
And always I shall feel time ravel thin about me.
For once I stood
In the white windy presence of eternity.

          —EUNICE TIETJENS

Look on these quiet mountains. Let our quest
    Be Nature's silences. Return the gaze
Of these all-seeing stars, till the still ways
Of the living wilderness restore life's zest.
These are our inner selves, made manifest
    In grandeur and serenity, that raise
The petty stature of our restless days
To match their own immensities of rest.

                —PERCY MACKAYE

And thus these threatening ranges of dark mountains, which, in nearly all ages of the world, men have looked upon with aversion or with terror, are, in reality, sources of life and happiness far fuller and more beneficent than the bright fruitfulness of the plain.

                —RUSKIN

Moraine of Ngojumba Glacier, due south of Cho Oyu

It did not come all at once, that sense of consuming solitude. At first it was just a matter of resting passively amidst spectacular scenery, but this steadily changed into a peculiarly mixed sensation of *aroused* relaxation; poised and attentive, infinitely at ease. After so much effort, to *sit* there—totally alone at 25,000 feet, surrounded by a still and motionless world of rock and ice and blue-black sky—was satisfying in a very special way. It was not the euphoria of altitude. It was the exhilaration of wilderness. Every feature of my surroundings gave evidence of violent force, yet all was calm and fixed—like a terrible battle scene suddenly frozen in a timeless tableau; the rock and ice polished by snow-blasting winds, the graceful sweep of flutings carved on the walls by avalanche, the grind and furor of the icefalls far below. But everything was silent and motionless . . . I remembered Hermann Buhl, and the lonely struggles he had so often won against his monstrous mountain opponent. Could he really have succumbed in this placid setting that surrounds him now? I raised my goggles for an unobstructed view of Beauty. That world of sharp and quiet contrasts became a sudden surge of undifferentiated silver light, bearing in on the interior of my skull from all directions, as though taking out a personal vengeance: "You would presume to see me as I really am!"

—RICHARD M. EMERSON

Unnamed peak above Thami en route to the pass of Tashi Lapcha

. . . our vivid and day-long consciousness of the mountain, of each other, and of the drama which we and the mountain played out at length together, cannot be faithfully reproduced. It has even escaped all but our own general recollection. The mountaineer returns to his hills because he remembers always that he has forgotten so much.

—GOEFFREY WINTHROP YOUNG

I am being driven forward
Into an unknown land.
The pass grows steeper,
The air colder and sharper.
A wind from my unknown goal
Stirs the strings
Of expectation.

Still the question:
Shall I ever get there?
There where life resounds,
A clear pure note
In the silence.

—DAG HAMMARSKJOLD

Kangtega (just showing) and Tamserku
Honga Peaks from near base of Ama Dablan

Flocks of birds have flown high and away.
A solitary drift of cloud, too, has gone, wandering on.
And I sit alone with the Ching-Ting Peak, towering beyond.
We never grow tired of each other, the mountain and I.

—LI PO (*d. 762*)

This grand show is eternal.
It is always sunrise somewhere:
the dew is never all dried at once:
*   a shower is forever falling, vapor is ever rising.*
Eternal sunrise, eternal sunset, eternal dawn and gloaming,
*   on sea and continents and islands, each in its turn,*
*   as the round earth rolls.*

—JOHN MUIR